THE SIDELINE HUSTLE

THE BLUEPRINT FOR BUILDING WEALTH BEHIND THE SCOREBOARD

TIERRE FORD

Copyright 2025 © by Tierre Ford

All rights reserved. No parts of this selection may be reproduced or transmitted in any form or by any means electronic or mechanical without permission in writing from publisher

Disclaimer

This book is a work of insight, experience, and research. The strategies, numbers, and examples presented are drawn from real-world observations and documented sources within the sports and business industries. While every effort has been made to provide accurate, practical, and inspiring content, results may vary based on individual effort, timing, circumstances, and application. This book is not a promise—it's a blueprint. Your success depends on how you build with it.

Tierre Ford

ABOUT THE AUTHOR

At just 12 years old, I started selling drugs in the 6th grade—following the blueprint I saw in my own home. My father was both a dealer and a user, and by the 7th grade, I had bought my first car, was paying my mama rent, and buying my own school clothes.

That same year, the school system labeled me as "slow." They placed me in a remedial reading class—embarrassed me, honestly. I was ashamed. But I still kept my swag, my gold chains, my Starter jackets, and my game face. I was one of the most popular kids in school, but truth be told, I had stopped learning. I was only there to show off.

Then one day, my reading teacher—who I'll never forget—looked me in my eyes and said, "You don't belong in this class. You're smart. Don't let them label you." Her words stuck with me, even though my CRT test scores said otherwise.

At age 12 years old I became my neighborhood's youngest drug supplier. I started with 10 dollars, and I flipped that all the way to over $500,000. Me and my Dad link up dealing together supplying the market. I dropped out of high school in the 10th grade. I bought my mother a house with a pool in the backyard, purchased luxury cars, before I was locked up at 19.

At that point in my life, I had never read a full book. Not one. But my father always told me, **"The mind is the most powerful tool in the universe. Street sense and book sense together? That's unstoppable."**

So I gave books a chance.

It started with street fiction. Then history. Then business. Then biographies about powerful and wealthy people. I started seeing myself in those pages—not always in their polish, but in their ambition, their boldness. Then I read **Think and Grow Rich and As a Man Thinketh.** Those two books changed my entire mindset.

That's when I met my friend Cool Harris. I saw some of his writing on a notepad, and it rocked my world. I realized I had something to say, too. From that moment on, I picked up the pencil—and I've never looked back.

I earned my GED, took business and college courses, and started studying resilience. I discovered that, back in the day, Black people were once forbidden to read. There's even a saying: **"If you want to hide something from a Black person, put it in a book."** That became my fuel.

Now, I write both fiction and self-help books, covering everything from mindset and mental toughness to financial strategy and spiritual growth. I pour my soul into every page with one mission: to light a fire inside someone who's ready for change.

To everyone who's followed my journey—thank you. Let's set the world on fire with truth, with courage, with knowledge. Let's break every chain and every myth that says we don't read.

Peace—And Keep The Faith.

TIERRE FORD

Tierre Ford

AUTHOR'S NOTE

This book wasn't written from theory. It was born from experience.

As a father of four boys, I've walked the long road of youth sports—the early morning practices, the weekend tournaments, the hopes, the wins, and the crushing letdowns. I've seen not just my own children, but countless others, pour their entire lives into a sport—only to hit that narrow window in college where opportunity fades and dreams stall.

Too many young athletes, and the parents who've sacrificed for them, end up feeling forgotten. Lost. Disappointed. But the truth is: **it was never just about playing the game.** It was always about how you position yourself around it.

There is *money in the margins*, *power in the sidelines*, and *generational wealth* in roles no one talks about. As you turn these pages, you'll see the billions generated in the world of sports—not just by the athletes, but by the ones who understand the business behind the ball.

This book is your wake-up call. Your blueprint. Your chance to stop hoping and start building.

Don't hope. Become it.
Don't chase the league. Own your lane.
There's wealth in this game—and your seat is waiting.

Tierre Ford

TABLE OF CONTENTS

Copyright _____ II
Author's Message _____ III

1. The Numbers Game — Why The Odds Matter _____ 1
2. From Dream To Data — Know The Field You're Playing On ___ 8
3. Football Money Is Everywhere — You Just Weren't Told _____ 14
4. 20+ Careers That Pay — $200k+ Without The Nfl _____ 22
5. The Compound Effect — How Small Moves Build Big Wins ___ 29
6. The Final Drive — Recap, Realignment, And The Story That Changed It All _____ 35
7. Beyond The Buzzer — How To Win In Basketball Without Going Pro _____ 39
8. Nil, Aau & Sneaker Politics — The Game Inside The Game ___ 47
9. 20+ Careers In Basketball That Pay — $200k And Beyond ____ 56
10. Her Game Is Global — How Female Athletes Are Owning The Court And The Check _____ 64
11. From The Sideline To The Stream — Fresh Ways To Make Money In Basketball _____ 69
12. Final Possession — Flip The Game, Don't Just Play It _____ 74
13. Diamonds And Data — Understanding The Baseball Pipeline __ 78
14. 20+ Baseball Careers That Pay — $200k And Beyond _____ 84
15. Start Where You Are — What You Can Do, What It Costs, And When To Begin _____ 89
16. The Baseball Revenue Map — How The Game Pays If You Know Where To Stand _____ 96

17. Diamonds & Deposits — How Softball Pays From College To Sunday League___102
18. Play On Purpose — Turning Passion Into Payment___108
19. Quiet Power — The Real Game Of Golf___112
20. Green On The Greens — How Golf Pays When You Play It Smart___117
21. Disrupt The Fairway — How To Make Money From Liv Golf Without Playing___124
22. Her Swing, Her Stage — How Women Are Changing The Game And The Business Of Golf___131
23. Bags, Boards & Belief — The Real Power In Golf That Pays For Life___137
24. The Compound Game — Stacking Swings, Stacking Wins___142
25. Behind The Racket — The Real Game Of Tennis From Youth To Pro___146
26. The Other Court — How To Make Money In Tennis Without Going Pro___150
27. Serve & Earn — The Real Revenue In Tennis And How To Tap In___157
28. The Pickleball Wave — History, Hustle, And The New Money Game___161
29. The Global Game — Inside The Numbers Of Soccer's Reach And Rise___166
30. The Other Goal — How To Make Money From Soccer Without Going Pro___170
31. Beyond The Pitch — Closing The Soccer Section With Power, Vision, And Legacy___175
32. Lanes Of Truth — The Track From Youth To Pro___179

33. From The Sideline — Where The Real Track Money Lives____185
34. Her Lane — Women, Mental Health, And Mindset In Track And Field____191
35. The Rise Of The Net — Inside The Numbers Of Volleyball's Climb____196
36. Over The Net — Making Money In Volleyball Without Going Pro____200
37. The Fight For The Dream — Breaking Down Boxing From Youth To Pro____205
38. Outside The Ring — The Blueprint To Eat Without Taking A Hit____211
39. Beyond The Bell — The Money In Ufc, Pro Wrestling, And The Hustle After The Hype____219
40. Motivational Speech: "Write Your Own Highlight Reel"____225
41. Plan Like A Boss — Building A Real Business Strategy____228
42. Fund The Hustle — Getting Capital Without Selling Your Soul____233
43. Build While Broke — The Compound Effect Of Daily Discipline____238
44. Market With Heart — Your Story Is Your Superpower____246
45. The Builder's Blueprint____249
46. Behind The Game — The Final Hustle Play____253

CHAPTER 1

The Numbers Game — Why The Odds Matter

"Dream big — but study the terrain before you charge. Because even lions pick the right battles."

From the first time a little boy laces up cleats, or a young girl tosses a football across a patch of grass, the dream begins:
The League.
The bright lights.
The roar of the crowd.
The contract that changes generations.

It's a beautiful dream — but if no one ever tells you the full story, it can also become a brutal trap.

Not because you're not talented.
Not because you don't want it badly enough.
But because the system was **never designed** to let most players win.

It's time we tell the truth, with love and precision.

This chapter isn't here to scare you — it's here to equip you.

Because real winners know: **you can still build an empire — you just have to see the whole field first.**

Starting Point: How Many Kids Play Football?

Let's begin with the raw numbers:

- **Pee Wee/Youth Football:**
  Over **1.2 million** kids under 14 play organized football in America each year.
- **High School Football:**
  Approximately **1,036,000** boys played high school football during the 2022–2023 season, according to the National Federation of State High School Associations (NFHS).
  (Girls' participation is rising too — about **3,900** girls nationwide.)
- **College Football:**
  Out of that million+ high school players:
  - **73,712** will go on to play **NCAA college football** (Divisions I, II, III combined).
    That's about **7%** of high school players.
- **NFL Draft Hopefuls:**
  Only about **1,600** draft-eligible players are seriously considered each year.
  - **259** players were selected in the 2023 NFL Draft.
  - **Approximately 1.6%** of college football players will make it to the NFL.

What Do These Numbers Really Mean?

Let's make it plain:

- For every 100 high school football players...
  7 will play in college.
  1 might make it to the NFL Combine.
  Even fewer will actually be drafted.
- For every **1,000** kids playing Pop Warner football today, **less than 2** will ever take a snap in the NFL.

And even for those who **do** make it:

- The **average NFL career lasts just 3.3 years.**
- Over **78% of NFL players** face serious financial trouble within **3 years of retirement** (per Sports Illustrated).

Translation:
The system is built like a funnel.
Wide at the bottom.
Narrow and brutal at the top.

The Injury Gauntlet

And then there's this:

Football is violent. It's part of the beauty — and the danger.

Here are real injury stats:

- **Every NFL game:** Players face a **100% probability of getting injured** over the course of their career.
- **Concussion rates:** 10-15% per season (and those are only the reported ones).
- **Knee injuries (ACL/MCL tears):** 40% of major football injuries.
- **High school injuries:** 1 out of every 3 high school players experiences a significant injury that affects playing time.

At every level — Pop Warner, JV, Varsity, College, Pros — injury is part of the ecosystem.

No one walks away untouched.

Why Odds And Stats Matter

Some will say:
"Don't tell these kids the numbers. You'll kill their dreams!"

No.
Telling the truth doesn't kill dreams.
It saves *lives*.
It gives players **options**.
It lets them dream *wider*.

If you know the real odds...
You can build **multiple wins** instead of gambling it all on one shot.

It's like a quarterback reading a defense:
If the deep ball is covered, you check down, you scramble, you *adjust*.

Champions adjust.
Losers blame the system later.

Football Is Bigger Than The Field

The key to surviving — and thriving — isn't abandoning football.

It's understanding that **football is a universe**, not just a goalpost.

Football is:

- A **$15+ billion** business annually.

- A machine that needs trainers, coaches, broadcasters, marketing experts, equipment designers, lawyers, data scientists, NIL managers, branding consultants, performance psychologists...

- A platform that can launch:
    - Clothing brands
    - Camps
    - Podcasts
    - Fitness programs
    - Youth leagues
    - Motivational speaking careers

If you love football — **you can still build your whole life around it** without sacrificing your future to a lottery ticket.

You just need the right playbook.

Mindset Shift: From Player To Producer

You are not just an athlete.
You are a **business**.
You are a **brand**.
You are a **system builder**.

Whether you go pro, coach, build, or manage... you can be part of the **game of football** without breaking your body or betting everything on one roll of the dice.

The real win isn't being drafted.
It's being **free**.
Financially.
Mentally.
Legacy-wise.

And freedom comes when you know **the game inside out** — not just between the lines.

Key Takeaways

- **Odds matter.** Knowing them makes you powerful, not weak.

- **Football is bigger than the field.** There are millions of dollars circulating beyond the turf.
- **You are a brand.** Start seeing yourself that way now.
- **Multiple dreams = multiple wins.** Stack your options.
- **Mindset first. Strategy second. Hustle third.**

Excellent question — and it's a powerful move.

Adding **"Spotlight Stories"** to your chapters gives the reader:

1. **Real-world proof** that this works.

2. **Inspiration** through example.

3. A **break from data-heavy reading**, with emotional storytelling.

Here's how you can do it **cleanly and consistently**:

How To Add "Spotlight Stories" To Chapters

1. Use a Consistent Format

Each Spotlight should have a **title, quick background, and emotional takeaway**. Keep it short but powerful (200–400 words).

2. Place it Between Sections or at the End

After a major section (like "Injury Stats" or "NFL Odds"), drop in a Spotlight as a real-world example. It reinforces the message just covered.

3. Use These Headings:

- **Spotlight:** [Name or Title]
- **Real Talk:** [Person's Quote]
- **Playbook Moment:** (Short bullet takeaway of what we can learn from their journey)

Spotlight: "The Quarterback Who Never Made It — But Built a $5M Business"

Name: *Tyrone Watson*
Hometown: *Jackson, Mississippi*
Dream: Go D1, get drafted, buy his mom a house.

Tyrone was *that dude* in high school — All-State quarterback, full-ride offer to a mid-tier D1 school. But a torn ACL sophomore year of college ended that dream fast. Instead of quitting, Tyrone pivoted.

He started helping younger players in his area rehab, train, and prepare for college. That became **Watson Elite Performance**, a training company that now operates out of 3 facilities in the South, trains over 300 athletes a year, and sells branded training gear nationwide.

Today, Tyrone makes well over $500K a year — **off football.** No draft. No helmet. Still winning.

Real Talk:
"I thought I lost everything when I tore my ACL. Turns out, I found my purpose. The game wasn't my path — it was my platform."

Playbook Moment:

- When one dream closes, build another from the rubble.
- Use what you know — and help the next wave win.
- Ownership > highlights.

"Don't just dream of playing in the game. Dream of owning the game."

Chapter 2

From Dream To Data — Know The Field You're Playing On

"A dream without data is like a quarterback with no film — loud potential, no direction."

So You Wanna Go All The Way...

Every Friday night, lights beam down on young athletes like stars fell from the sky.
Crowds chant.
Uniforms shine.
And somewhere in those stands, a parent or coach is whispering:

"He got next."

But while everybody's watching the highlight play, nobody's checking the reality stats.
 And without **clarity**, dreams become traps.

This chapter is about **seeing the field for what it really is** — not just what you hope it might be.
 Because if you truly love football, you need to understand the **ecosystem** — not just the end zone.

The Football Funnel: From Pee-Wee To Pro

Football has always felt like a ladder.
But in truth, it's a funnel.
Wide at the bottom. Narrow at the top. And **millions** fall off along the way.

Let's Walk It (Football Funnel Breakdown –

- **Youth Football (Pee Wee / Pop Warner):**
  Over **1.2 million kids** under 14 play organized youth football each year in the U.S.
- **High School Football:**
  About **1,036,000** high school boys play football each season (NFHS data).
    - Out of these, **only about 7%** will go on to play in college.
- **College Football (All NCAA Divisions):**
  Around **73,700 players** total across Division I, II, and III.
    - Of those, **only about 1.6%** will make it to the NFL.
- **NFL Draft Hopefuls:**
  Roughly **1,600 players** are considered "draft eligible" each year.
    - Only **259 are drafted** (2023 stats).
    - That's less than **2%** of college players making it to the pros.
- **NFL Roster Spots:**
  There are **1,696 active roster spots** (32 teams × 53-man rosters).
    - The competition for those spots is global.
- **Average NFL Career Length:**
  The average NFL player career lasts just **3.3 years**.

Now zoom in:
- Out of **1 million high school players**, only about **7 in 100** play in college.

- From there, **only 1–2 players out of every 100** college players get drafted.
- Most players — **even stars** — never play beyond college.
- Many don't even finish their college career due to injury, burnout, or grades.

This is not negativity.
This is **clarity.**
And clarity is power.

The Pressure Trap: Why Tunnel Vision Destroys Potential

One of the most dangerous lies in youth sports is this:

"You either make it, or you failed."

That mindset has sent thousands of boys and girls into depression, anxiety, and lifelong regret — all because they believed the only path to success wore a jersey.

Here's what tunnel vision does:

- Ignores other talents
- Makes you fear Plan B
- Kills curiosity
- Destroys flexibility
- Ties your value to performance

Result: You start living *for the field*, and not *from the field*.

But when you zoom out?
You realize the field is just the start — not the destination.

A Better Lens: The Full Football Ecosystem

Here's what most people don't realize:
Football isn't just about players.
It's a **global economy.**

And every team, every stadium, every media deal... *needs people to run it.*

Let's Reframe What Success Looks Like (Football Roles –

Here are real examples of success in football that don't require putting on pads:
- **High School Coach**
    - *Impact:* Player development, leadership, community builder
    - *Estimated Pay:* $50K–$120K+
- **Recruiting Analyst**
    - *Impact:* Scouting and rating high school/college talent
    - *Estimated Pay:* $60K–$200K+
- **Sports Agent**
    - *Impact:* Negotiating deals and protecting athletes
    - *Estimated Pay:* $100K–$1M+
- **Team Logistics Director**
    - *Impact:* Manages travel, gear, scheduling, and operations
    - *Estimated Pay:* $80K–$250K+
- **NIL Consultant**
    - *Impact:* Helps athletes monetize name, image, and likeness
    - *Estimated Pay:* $100K–$400K+
- **Athletic Trainer**
    - *Impact:* Keeps players healthy and injury-free
    - *Estimated Pay:* $75K–$180K+
- **Sports Broadcaster / Commentator**
    - *Impact:* Tells the story of the game on TV or radio
    - *Estimated Pay:* $70K–$500K+
- **Equipment Brand Owner**

- ○ *Impact:* Creates gear and swag that players wear
- ○ *Estimated Pay:* Varies — some earn 6–7 figures

This is just a sample.
The football world is deep.
It has **layers, sectors, rooms you've never even seen.**
And you can eat well in every one of them.

Mindset Shift: Own More Than Your Position

Football players are trained to master **positioning**.
But now it's time to master **positioning in life.**

Ask yourself:

- What else do I love about the game?
- Can I lead? Teach? Strategize? Market? Build community?
- Am I more than just fast? More than strong?
- Can I build a brand? Host a show? Start a camp?

You don't have to choose between being passionate and being paid.

The truth is:
Passion pays — when it's directed with purpose.

How To Start Seeing The Bigger Picture

1. **Study the business of football**
   - ○ Read about sports marketing, team ownership, NIL trends
2. **Talk to people in other roles**
   - ○ Ask your trainer, ask your coach's assistant, follow team managers on social media
3. **Build a secondary skill**
   - ○ Editing video, public speaking, entrepreneurship, writing, photography
4. **Volunteer or shadow**
   - ○ Help run a youth camp, keep stats for a game, offer to film practices

5. **Ask better questions**
    - Not "How do I make the league?"
    - But "How do I win *from* the league — even if I never play a down?"

Spotlight Story: The Equipment Guy Who Became A Ceo

Name: *Jordan Matthews*
Hometown: *Flint, Michigan*
Dream: D1 football. But he barely made varsity.
Jordan loved football — but he wasn't built for the next level.
So instead of quitting the game, he asked to work with the team staff.
He became the **equipment assistant**, then earned a part-time job in college helping fit players with gear.
One day, frustrated with the lack of cool cleat covers and compression gear, Jordan started sketching designs.
Today, his brand **"Gripline Athletics"** is worn by players in **over 60 colleges and 8 NFL teams**.
He never ran a 4.4.
Never lifted 225 on bench for reps.
But he made the game *his business*.
Real Talk:
"My hands were never the fastest, but my ideas were. And now my name still gets called on Sundays — just on shoes, not scoreboards."
Playbook Moment:
- Stay close to the game, even if the position changes
- Build something that serves the athletes
- Every locker room has million-dollar problems waiting for a solution

"If the field is the only place you see opportunity, you're missing the whole stadium."

Chapter 3

Football Money Is Everywhere — You Just Weren't Told

"Don't just chase the ball. Chase the business behind it."

The Truth They Don't Put In The Playbook

For most athletes, football starts with a ball and a dream.

But behind every touchdown is a ticket.
Behind every helmet is a brand.
Behind every championship is a budget.

Football isn't just a sport.
It's a **$15 billion** American industry — and that's just on paper. If you include youth camps, streetwear, NIL deals, YouTube creators, and brand partnerships? You're looking at a **$20–30 billion ecosystem.**

The game has **so much more money around it than in it** — and yet most young players only see one door:

Play or go home.

Let's change that now.

This chapter breaks down **how the money flows** at **each level** — from high school all the way to the pros — and how you can position yourself **to get paid** without ever taking a snap on TV.

High School Level: The Ground Floor Of Football Business

You might think high school football is small-time.
But the machine is already moving — and people are already eating.

Where's the Money? (High School Football Level –

Here are real ways people earn money around high school football — even without being on the field:

- Private Trainers
    - What They Do: Run speed, agility, or position-specific drills
    - Pay: $50 to $150 per hour
- **Videographers / Media Editors**
    - What They Do: Create highlight reels, game recaps, recruiting content
    - Pay: $200 to $1,000 per player or project
- **7-on-7 Organizers**
    - What They Do: Run offseason tournaments and travel teams
    - Pay: $5,000 to $100,000 per season (depending on scale and sponsors)
- **Referees / Game Officials**
    - What They Do: Officiate games at middle and high school levels

        ○ Pay: $60 to $150 per game
- **Gear Retailers / Merch Designers**
        ○ What They Do: Sell gloves, mouthguards, shirts, team-branded gear
        ○ Pay: Varies (some side hustles earn thousands per season)
- **Social Media Managers**
        ○ What They Do: Help players or teams build Instagram, YouTube, or Twitter presence
        ○ Pay: $25 to $100 per hour (or monthly retainers)

Real Talk:
Parents spend thousands a year on gear, travel, trainers, and exposure.
 That's not a problem — it's a signal:
 People are willing to pay for better football experiences.
If you're 16 with a camera and editing skills? You can start a highlight reel business TODAY.
 If you're 18 and know how to coach footwork? You can launch position-specific clinics for youth players.
You don't need a degree — you need value.

College Level: The Golden Window (Especially With NIL)

College football is where the money multiplies.

What Changed Everything: NIL

Before July 2021, college athletes couldn't make money off their name.
 Now? It's a wide-open game.

- **Top college players are earning six figures** — not from the NCAA, but from brands, YouTube, merch, and camps.
- **NIL Agencies and consultants** are popping up daily.
- **Media creators** are building entire platforms around recruiting and athlete stories.

Where's The Money? (College Football Level –

At the college level, the business side of football gets bigger — and the money gets real. Here are some roles and how they pay:

- **NIL Consultant**
    - What They Do: Help athletes land sponsorships, manage deals, and understand compliance
    - Pay: $100,000 to $400,000+ (often percentage-based)
- **Team Nutritionist**
    - What They Do: Create custom meal plans and diets for peak athletic performance
    - Pay: $75,000 to $150,000+
- **Player Development Staff**
    - What They Do: Mentor athletes, teach life skills, help with off-the-field success
    - Pay: $60,000 to $120,000
- **Creative Media Team**
    - What They Do: Handle game graphics, edits, recruiting visuals, hype videos
    - Pay: $40,000 to $100,000 (some go higher with experience)
- **Sports Information Directors (SIDs)**
    - What They Do: Manage media relations, stats, and team communications
    - Pay: $60,000 to $140,000+
- **Academic Advisors for Athletics**
    - What They Do: Help athletes stay eligible and graduate
    - Pay: $60,000 to $90,000+
- **College Recruiting Coordinators / Analysts**

- What They Do: Track and evaluate high school talent, manage the recruiting board
- Pay: $60,000 to $150,000+

BONUS: If you're a former player? Start position-specific Zoom clinics, run mental toughness webinars, or sell recruiting eBooks.

You can run your entire business from your phone, if you're intentional.

Pro Level: The Billion-Dollar Battlefield

Once you hit the league, the money is massive — but again, it's not just for players.

Where's the Money? (Pro Football Level – Clean Format)

At the pro level, football becomes a corporate machine — and the people making the money often aren't the ones in uniform. Here are some of the top roles and their pay:

- Sports Agent
  - What They Do: Negotiate player contracts, brand deals, and endorsements
  - Pay: $150,000 to $2,000,000+ (based on player contracts and commissions)
- Athletic Trainers / Performance Staff
  - What They Do: Keep players healthy, rehab injuries, and improve performance
  - Pay: $100,000 to $300,000+
- **Front Office Executives (GM, Player Personnel, Ops)**
  - What They Do: Oversee team strategy, roster building, and business decisions
  - Pay: $90,000 to $500,000+ (senior positions can reach 7 figures)
- **Content Creators / Influencers (NFL-focused)**
  - What They Do: Cover games, react to plays, build digital sports brands

- Pay: Unlimited — some earn $5,000 to $50,000+ per month via ads, sponsors, merch
- **Brand Managers (Athlete-Focused)**
  - What They Do: Build and manage the public image, marketing strategy, and social media presence for pro athletes
  - Pay: $100,000 to $250,000+
- **App Developers / Fantasy Sports Tools**
  - What They Do: Build products, platforms, or tools around the pro football experience
  - Pay: Varies — can range from small SaaS to multi-million-dollar startups

Let's Be Clear:
You may never catch a pass on Sunday.
But you can run a company that serves those who do.
And some of them will write you checks bigger than their own signing bonuses.

New School Hustles (Digital Football Economy)

Let's talk 2024 and beyond:
- **YouTube Football Creators** — covering film, recruiting, stories
- **Podcast Hosts** — breaking down games, interviewing players
- **eBooks + Online Courses** — "How to Get Noticed in HS Football"
- **Football Clothing Brands** — gloves, hoodies, slogans
- **Affiliate Marketing** — repping gear & getting paid per sale
- **Digital Trainers** — Zoom footwork sessions, virtual coaching

These are REAL lanes.
Some 19-year-olds are making $200K/year off YouTube by talking about football intelligently and consistently.

Why Most People Miss It

Because no one told them to look.

- Schools push traditional careers.
- Coaches push the field.
- Parents push scholarships.
- But **no one pushes ownership.**

That's where you come in.

You don't have to ask permission to build.
You just have to be **consistent, sharp, and valuable.**

How To Find Your Lane In Football's Business

Ask yourself:

- Do I like being on camera? → YouTube/Media
- Do I love training others? → Private sessions, clinics
- Do I understand branding? → Start an NIL agency
- Do I like fashion? → Build a brand with a football culture
- Am I organized? → Team ops, logistics, camp director
- Am I strategic? → Recruiting, player development, consulting

Then go test it.

Don't wait for someone to say, "You got potential."
Show them you've got **product.**

Spotlight Story: From Jv To Media Mogul

Name: Chad "Coach C" Walker
Hometown: Newark, NJ
Dream: Go D1. Reality? He didn't start varsity until senior year. No offers.
Instead of giving up on football, Chad started **breaking down film** on Instagram.

At first, no one watched.
But he kept going.
He started giving honest advice, calling out common mistakes, and helping parents understand the process.
Fast forward 3 years:
- **Coach C Football** is now a full media brand
- 50K+ IG followers
- 100+ clients trained annually
- Hosts showcases for unsigned seniors
- Last year, **he cleared $210K** in training, brand deals, and media packages

Real Talk:
"I thought I failed when I didn't go D1. But I didn't fail — I found a better lane."

Playbook Moment:
- You don't need a whistle to be a coach.
- You don't need a scout to be a voice.
- The game is bigger when you build it yourself.

"The money in football isn't locked in the scoreboard — it's hidden in the sidelines, stories, and systems. Go find it."

Chapter 4

20+ Careers That Pay — $200K+ Without the NFL

"You don't need to be on the field to make money from the game — you just need to be in the room where the plays are made."

Let's Be Clear: Playing Is One Position. Ownership Is Another.

When you really understand football, you stop thinking like a player — and start thinking like a **producer**.

You see the full structure:

- Who runs the team?
- Who cuts the deals?
- Who manages the schedule?
- Who builds the brand?
- Who counts the money?
- Who controls the film?

Every role exists for a reason — and the paychecks reflect that.

Below are **20+ careers** where football connects to **real wealth**, with **clear paths** to $200K+ per year.

Some you can start today.

Others take years to build.

But all of them are **real**.

1. Sports Agent

What They Do: Negotiate contracts, manage deals, protect clients
Pay Range: $100K to $2M+ (commission-based)
How to Start: Law or business degree + agent certification + network like crazy
Why It Works: You earn a % of your client's deal — and some players want a rep who understands their background

Play smarter. Talk harder. Be their voice.

2. NIL Manager / Consultant

What They Do: Help college players land legal brand deals
Pay Range: $100K–$400K+
How to Start: Marketing background, strong social media skills, learn NCAA NIL rules
Why It Works: NIL is exploding — players need guidance, especially from people who've been in their shoes

Most players don't need an agent yet — they need someone who understands the new money game.

3. Athletic Performance Trainer

What They Do: Develop speed, strength, recovery routines
Pay Range: $70K–$250K+ (top earners make 7 figures)
How to Start: Get certified (NASM, CSCS), start training youth players, post your results
Why It Works: Great trainers get referrals nonstop — especially if they build relationships with local coaches

Your program is your product. Your players are your promotion.

4. Private Position Coach

What They Do: Work 1-on-1 or with small groups by position (QB, WR, DB, etc.)
Pay Range: $50/hr up to $200K+/yr
How to Start: Play the position, coach it, build film clips, get referrals
Why It Works: Parents pay top dollar for "next level" development

If you know what a scout looks for, teach that. Then teach it better than anyone else.

5. Brand Consultant (Athletes)

What They Do: Build image, logos, websites, media packages for players
Pay Range: $80K–$300K
How to Start: Learn Canva, storytelling, brand psychology, and how athletes think
Why It Works: The next LeBron might be 16 years old. Help him look like a pro before he becomes one.

6. YouTube Football Creator

What They Do: Break down film, create stories, react to highlights, review gear
Pay Range: Unlimited (Some earn $5K–$40K/mo)
How to Start: Phone, niche topic, consistent uploads
Why It Works: Sports content never dies. If you're real and consistent, the views and sponsors will come.

Tell the story no one else is telling — and own your lane.

7. College Recruiting Analyst

What They Do: Help schools scout talent, rate athletes, provide insights
Pay Range: $60K–$200K+
How to Start: Watch film, build your own rankings, join Rivals/247Sports/On3 platforms

Why It Works: Great analysts build trust with both coaches and families

8. Football Data Analyst / Statistician

What They Do: Use data to help teams make smarter decisions
Pay Range: $90K–$250K
How to Start: Excel + sports knowledge + coding (Python/R) = elite combo
Why It Works: Analytics run front offices now. Be fluent in football and numbers, and you'll never be jobless.

9. Team Operations Manager

What They Do: Handle logistics, travel, schedules, housing, gear
Pay Range: $75K–$200K
How to Start: Intern with a college program or NFL team, build relationships
Why It Works: Coaches trust the person who runs the details. That role is often gold behind the scenes.

10. Sports Psychologist (Performance Mindset Coach)

What They Do: Help athletes stay mentally sharp, reduce anxiety, focus under pressure
Pay Range: $90K–$250K+
How to Start: Psych degree + sports certification + internships
Why It Works: Mental health is finally being taken seriously in sports — and players will pay for real results.

11. Sports Apparel Entrepreneur

What They Do: Design and sell sports-inspired gear (shirts, gloves, hoodies, cleats)
Pay Range: Unlimited
How to Start: Simple logo + Shopify store + content + consistency
Why It Works: If your gear tells a story people relate to, they'll buy it — and tell others

12. Football Camp Director / Showcase Host

What They Do: Organize and run events to showcase players' skills
Pay Range: $10K–$200K+/season (based on size, sponsors, entry fees)
How to Start: Start local with trusted coaches. Offer what camps don't.
Why It Works: Players need exposure. Parents pay for opportunity.

13. Sports Broadcaster / Commentator

What They Do: Call games, host shows, break news
Pay Range: $60K–$1M+
How to Start: Local high school games, IG/YouTube clips, podcasting
Why It Works: If your voice stands out, the audience grows. Then the money follows.

14. Referee / Officiating Crew Member

What They Do: Officiate games (HS, college, pro)
Pay Range: $40K–$200K+ (NFL refs make up to $250K/year)
How to Start: Take certification courses, start with youth/HS
Why It Works: Every game needs one. And if you're fair, consistent, and sharp — you'll move up.

15. Sports Lawyer / Contract Advisor

What They Do: Handle endorsement deals, contracts, disputes
Pay Range: $120K–$400K+
How to Start: Law school + sports management connections
Why It Works: Every pro athlete eventually needs legal help. If they trust you, they'll keep you.

16. Financial Advisor (Athletes)

What They Do: Help players manage money, invest, avoid scams
Pay Range: $100K–$500K+

How to Start: Finance license + deep trust
Why It Works: 78% of NFL players go broke after retirement. You could help change that.

17. Equipment Specialist / Custom Fitter

What They Do: Fit and modify gear for performance + safety
Pay Range: $60K–$120K+
How to Start: Intern with team staff, study gear tech
Why It Works: Teams invest in every edge. If you make players feel better, move better — you get paid.

18. Virtual Skills Coach

What They Do: Offer breakdowns, footwork training, drills via Zoom
Pay Range: $50–$150/hr
How to Start: Build curriculum, get testimonials, market online
Why It Works: Some kids live in places with no elite trainers — but they have Wi-Fi.

19. Motivational Speaker / Author

What They Do: Teach lessons from football through speeches and books
Pay Range: $1,000–$25,000/speech
How to Start: Tell your story, build a speaking reel, network
Why It Works: Real stories = real impact = real checks

20. Sports Media Editor / Designer

What They Do: Create graphics, film cuts, visual content
Pay Range: $50K–$150K+
How to Start: Learn Canva, Adobe, or CapCut. Start posting.
Why It Works: Every team, brand, and player needs to look good online. Be the one who makes that happen.

Tierre Ford

Spotlight Story: From Second-String To Six Figures

Name: Levi "Vizualz" Carter
Hometown: Charlotte, NC
Dream: Start at DB. Never did.

Levi loved football, but he was never the fastest or strongest.
He rode the bench most of high school.
But what he could do?
Edit videos.

He started cutting highlight reels for teammates.
Then coaches.
Then local teams.
Fast forward 5 years:

- He now runs **Vizualz Football Media**
- Edits content for top recruits and Power 5 schools
- Just signed a retainer deal with an NIL agency
- 2023 income: $235K

Real Talk:
"I wanted to make the field. Instead, I made a living. And now I'm on every screen — even if I never touched the ball."

Playbook Moment:

- If your talent's not athletic, make it creative.
- Every story needs a storyteller.
- The game doesn't care where you start — only what you build.

"You don't need a number on your jersey to leave a legacy in the game. Just a skill — and the courage to use it "

Chapter 5

The Compound Effect — How Small Moves Build Big Wins

"You don't have to move fast. You just have to move forward — every single day."

Why Some Players Win After The Whistle Blows

Ever wonder why one athlete with average stats becomes a millionaire...while another with freakish talent fades into silence?

It's not always skill.
It's not always luck.
It's often **compound movement** — a series of small, smart choices made over time that stack up to greatness.

This is **the compound effect.**

It's the difference between hype and habits.
Between having a dream... and building one.

What Is The Compound Effect?

Coined by entrepreneur Darren Hardy, the compound effect is simple:

Small actions, done consistently, over time = massive results.

You won't see the fruit at first.
That's the trap.

- One video won't blow you up.
- One offseason won't get you scouted.
- One networking email won't land you a job.

But day after day?
That's where the magic lives.

This isn't theory.
This is real.
Especially in football and business.

Let's Talk Football: How Compound Wins Really Work

The Player Example:

- **Freshman year:** You film your own drills. No likes.
- **Sophomore year:** You post twice a week. Start tagging coaches.
- **Junior year:** You edit your highlights. Clean brand. 1K followers.
- **Senior year:** A D3 school sees your hustle and offers. Boom.

The kid who waited on exposure never got noticed.
The one who worked his brand daily?
He got in.

The Business Example

- **You're 20:** You start training one 8th grader in your backyard.
- **Next month:** Two more show up. You charge $20.
- **6 months later:** You post their results on IG. Get 12 new kids.

- **By 22:** You're running a $4K/month side business off drills. Nothing fancy.
 Just effort + time + consistency.

Why Most People Quit Before The Breakthrough

Because they want the crowd, not the craft.

They post three times. No response.
They train four clients. No referrals.
They try to build something — and it takes longer than expected.

So they walk away.

Not realizing they were **inches from the blessing**.

The compound effect isn't loud.
It's quiet.
Steady.
Patient.
And absolutely lethal when you believe in it.

Stacking Your Small Wins

Here's how small, consistent actions in football and business stack into real momentum over time:

- **Post drills or training clips (2x per week)**
  Builds social proof, attracts attention, and earns referrals
- **Study the business of sports (30 minutes a day)**
  Gives you a competitive edge and smarter long-term vision
- **Reach out to one new connection weekly (email, DM, or in person)**
  Expands your network and opens new doors over time
- **Run a youth camp or private session (monthly)**
  Builds your brand, reputation, and an additional income stream

- **Read one book per month on leadership, sports, or business**
    Grows your mindset and sharpens your skills
- **Save or reinvest $25 per week**
    Results in over $1,300 a year for tools, gear, or business moves

Here's what stacking looks like in real life:
Small steps.
Big gains.
You don't need to be perfect — just **present** and **persistent**.

How To Stay Locked In

1. **Keep score privately**
    Don't wait on applause. Track your consistency. Log your moves. Be your own scoreboard.

2. **Build a routine, not a reaction**
    Don't wait for motivation. Build structure:
    - Mondays = learning
    - Wednesdays = creating
    - Fridays = outreach

3. **Stay around energy**
    The wrong crowd will make you question every step. The right ones will remind you the vision takes time.

4. **Celebrate micro-wins**
    First 100 followers? That's a win.
    First parent thanks you for helping their kid? That's a win.
    First time someone asks "Do you do this full-time?" — **that's the sign.**

Real Compound Wins In The Football World

These are real examples of how consistent, compound action — not hype — leads to real wins in the football ecosystem:

- **Coach D**
    - What he did: Posted weekly linebacker breakdowns on YouTube
    - The result: Now runs a training facility and a NIL consulting business helping parents and players understand the new college landscape.
- **"Catch1st" Brand**
    - What they did: Dropped football-themed slogan hoodies monthly on Instagram
    - The result: Built a 6-figure streetwear brand that now sponsors 7-on-7 teams and hosts pop-up events at high school showcases.
- **QFilm Edits**
    - What he did: Edited 1–2 highlight videos per week for high school players
    - The result: Now works with D1 and D2 athletes, charges $250–$500 per edit, and earns $10K+ per month during recruiting season.
- **Jasmine Bryant**
    - What she did: Volunteered to coach girls' flag football every weekend
    - The result: Became a respected leader in youth football, now speaks at Nike Leadership Summits and consults on girls' football programs.

They didn't wait to be drafted.
They **drafted themselves** — one post, one drill, one session at a time.

Spotlight Story: The Player Who Didn't Play — But Still Won

Name: Erica Daniels
Hometown: Columbus, Ohio

Dream: Play safety in college. Never made varsity. Too small. Too quiet.

But Erica loved **watching film.**
Loved **noticing tendencies.**
So she started messaging youth coaches in her area — asking if they needed help breaking down tape.

Most ignored her.
One gave her a shot.

Today?

- She's the **Director of Player Analytics** at a JUCO program.
- Runs a private scouting service for under-the-radar athletes.
- Built a following of 15,000+ on Twitter for her weekly "Hidden Gems" report.
- Made over **$225,000 last year** through coaching, partnerships, and consulting.

Real Talk:
"I thought I was on the outside looking in. I didn't realize I could build my own entrance."

Playbook Moment:

- Your obsession isn't random.
- Your gift may not be flashy — but it's useful.
- Consistency makes the invisible, visible.

"Compound your effort, not your excuses. The world rewards what it can count."

Chapter 6

The Final Drive — Recap, Realignment, and the Story That Changed It All

"It's not about where football takes you. It's about what it leaves inside you — and what you do with it."

You've Seen The Game. Now It's Time To Run It.

If you've made it this far, you're not like everybody else.

You're not just playing to play.
You're thinking.
Learning.
Building.

You now understand that **football isn't just a field. It's an economy. A machine. A platform. A classroom. A mirror. A launchpad.**

And it's **your responsibility** to choose how you move inside it.

Because whether or not you go D1…
Whether or not your name gets called on draft day…
You can still win.

Let's Recap The Entire Football Playbook:

Chapter 1: The Numbers Game

- The odds of going pro are slim. The stats are real.
- But knowledge of the system makes you powerful.

Chapter 2: From Dream to Data

- Football is more than positions. It's a business.
- You have to zoom out and see the whole structure. That's how you find your lane.

Chapter 3: Football Money Is Everywhere

- There's money at every level — high school, college, and pro.
- Trainers, videographers, NIL consultants, camp creators — they're all part of the industry.

Chapter 4: 20+ Careers That Pay

- $200K+ jobs are already inside the game.
- Some need degrees. Others need grind. But they're all **real and reachable**.

Chapter 5: The Compound Effect

- The key isn't speed. It's consistency.
- You don't blow up — you build up.
- Your habits create your highlight reel.

And Now... The Story That Changes Everything

Spotlight: Inky Johnson — The Hit That Changed Everything

Tierre Ford

Name: Inquoris "Inky" Johnson
Hometown: Atlanta, Georgia
Position: Cornerback, University of Tennessee
Dream: NFL starter. Future millionaire.

Inky came from **nothing** — two-bedroom apartment with 14 people.
He worked. He studied. He trained until midnight.
He got his shot.

Game vs Air Force. September 9, 2006.
One tackle. Routine play.

Sudden impact.
He couldn't move his right arm.
Never would again.

Nerve damage. Career over. Just like that.

But instead of crumbling, Inky **transformed**.

- Got his master's in psychology
- Became a world-class motivational speaker
- Built a platform that reaches **millions**
- Now inspires CEOs, athletes, and young men around the world

Inky didn't just "bounce back."
He built **purpose** out of pain.
He turned a paralyzing hit into powerful healing.

Inky's Words:
"I lost the game... but I found my why."

So... What Will You Do With What You've Learned?

The game doesn't owe you anything.
But it gave you something:

- Discipline
- Toughness
- Vision
- Drive

That's more than enough to start **a business**
A platform. A movement. A future.

You know the blueprint now.

The rest is execution.

"Some play the game. Some coach it. Some own it. Decide which one you want to be — and move like it."

"You don't have to go pro to go powerful."

"The helmet was never the goal. The freedom was."

Chapter 7

Beyond the Buzzer — How to Win in Basketball Without Going Pro

"Talent might get you in the gym, but information is what gets you in the building where deals are made."

The Dream Is Real... But So Are The Odds

Basketball is one of the most pursued dreams in the world.

From driveways to summer leagues, rec centers to AAU tournaments, the hunger to "make it to the league" is in every city, every gym, every generation.

But let's break down the **real numbers** behind the dream — not to kill the fire, but to give it **direction.**

The Numbers Behind The Net (Basketball Funnel)

Let's break down the reality behind the dream of going pro in basketball:

- **U.S. High School Boys Basketball Players:**
  Approximately 540,000 boys play high school basketball each year.

- **College Basketball (NCAA Men's – All Divisions):**
  Around 18,000 players compete across Divisions I, II, and III.
  Only about 3.5% of high school players will go on to play college basketball.

- **Players Going Pro (NBA or Overseas):**
  Only about 1.2% of NCAA men's basketball players will make it to the professional level, including overseas leagues.

- **NBA Roster Spots:**
  The NBA has 450 total roster spots (30 teams × 15 players). Only 60 players are drafted each year, and not all stick on rosters.

- **Average NBA Career Length:**
  The average NBA career lasts approximately 4.5 years.

- **WNBA (Women's Basketball):**
  There are only 144 roster spots total across 12 teams.
  The competition is even more intense and limited on the women's side.

Translation:

- For every 10,000 high school players, **35 play in college**.

- Of those, only **1 or 2 will make the NBA or overseas rosters**.

And that's if you stay healthy, academically eligible, and perform at the highest level.

On the women's side, the odds are even smaller — with **144 total WNBA roster spots** in the world.

The Myth Of The Only Way

Basketball culture is loud about one thing:

"League or nothing."
That mindset has robbed too many players of seeing the bigger court — the **full ecosystem of the game**.

What we don't tell kids:

- You can **build a business** through basketball.
- You can **create wealth** without ever getting drafted.
- You can train, teach, design, report, broadcast, mentor, or lead from any corner of the court — if you know how.

And that's what this chapter is about.

Basketball's Revenue Ecosystem

Basketball isn't just a game. It's an **industry**.

The NBA alone made **$10.58 billion** in revenue in 2023. That doesn't include:

- College hoops
- AAU tournaments
- NIL deals
- Overseas leagues
- Streetwear brands
- Private trainers
- Skill camps
- Digital creators

Where there's attention, there's income.

Ways To Win Without Playing Pro

Let's break it down:

You don't need an NBA contract to make serious money in basketball. Here are some real, reachable roles with strong income potential:

- **Private Trainer**
    - What They Do: Work with youth, high school, college, or pro players on specific basketball skills
    - Estimated Pay: $60/hour to $250K+ per year
- **AAU Program Director**
    - What They Do: Manage youth basketball teams, tournaments, travel, and player exposure
    - Estimated Pay: $50K to $200K+ (depending on sponsorships and success)
- **NIL Brand Agent**
    - What They Do: Manage athletes' name, image, and likeness deals (especially college players)
    - Estimated Pay: $100K to $500K+ (commission-based or salaried)
- **Digital Creator**
    - What They Do: Post basketball content on YouTube, TikTok, Instagram — from breakdowns to storytelling
    - Estimated Pay: Unlimited potential — some earn $5K to $50K+ per month
- **Recruiting Analyst**
    - What They Do: Evaluate talent, track rankings, and provide scouting services to colleges or media outlets
    - Estimated Pay: $60K to $150K+
- **Basketball Apparel Founder**
    - What They Do: Create and sell basketball-themed clothing, shoes, accessories

- - Estimated Pay: Unlimited — depends on brand growth and sales strategy
- **Skills Coach (Virtual or In-Person)**
  - What They Do: Offer training via Zoom or in person for footwork, IQ, conditioning
  - Estimated Pay: $100/hour or more — 6 figures possible with high client load
- **College Coach (Staff)**
  - What They Do: Support players in development, academics, recruiting, or strategy
  - Estimated Pay: $50K to $250K+ (varies by program)
- **Pro Player Manager**
  - What They Do: Handle logistics, media, scheduling, and personal needs for professional players
  - Estimated Pay: $80K to $200K+
- **Sports Photographer / Videographer**
  - What They Do: Create highlight reels, game visuals, and social media content
  - Estimated Pay: $200 to $2,000+ per client or project
- **Tournament Host / League Organizer**
  - What They Do: Create and run local events, leagues, and exposure camps
  - Estimated Pay: $5K to $100K+ per event
- **Psychologist or Mental Performance Coach**
  - What They Do: Help players handle pressure, focus, and mindset
  - Estimated Pay: $80K to $220K+

Just like with football:

The players are only part of the court. The money lives in every corner.

Basketball Mindset: From Highlight To Hustle

The problem with hoop culture is that it's addicted to the moment:

- The dunk
- The buzzer beater
- The mixtape going viral

But most people lose when they stop chasing growth and start chasing applause.

Here's how to shift your mindset:

1. Fall in love with your lane — not the camera.
2. Use your basketball knowledge to solve problems for others.
3. Turn your journey into content, service, or leadership.
4. Study the game behind the game.

Stack Small Wins In The Basketball Space

Here's how to build long-term success through consistent, small moves in the basketball world:

- **Study one NCAA or NBA coaching system each week**
  Improves strategic thinking and prepares you for coaching or advanced play

- **Post one basketball training tip on social media each week**
  Builds your personal brand and shows value to players, parents, or sponsors

- **Attend at least one youth event or clinic each month**
  Expands your network, builds relationships, and keeps you visible in the community

- **Edit one highlight mixtape per player**
  Builds your media business and gives players real tools for exposure

- **Teach one basketball drill to a younger athlete whenever possible**
  Grows trust, develops your teaching ability, and leads to long-term referrals

- **Read one basketball-related business or leadership story every month**
  Keeps you sharp, inspired, and aware of new lanes and opportunities

The key? Same as football:
Consistency + Creativity = Opportunity.

Spotlight Story: From DNP To Division Builder

Name: Antonio "Tone" Harris
Hometown: Lithonia, Georgia
Dream: Play pro ball. Couldn't crack rotation in JUCO. Cut after freshman year.

Tone was crushed. No offers. No plan B.
But he started helping the team manager film practice.
He had an eye for spacing, timing, development.

That led to:

- A volunteer job helping run youth tournaments
- That turned into launching his own Atlanta-based youth league
- That led to building a player development program called **"WorkWins"**
- That led to camps, brand deals, trainers joining

- Now he makes over **$180K/year** — and just signed a contract to run a showcase with ESPN2 coverage

Real Talk:

"I didn't make the squad. So I built my own court."

Playbook Moment:

- Failure isn't the end — it's the fork.
- Love the game? Build from it.
- The best revenge is turning closed doors into your own gym.

"Some people play the game. Others build the court."

"Basketball doesn't owe you anything. But it gave you everything you need to win."

"You are the brand. You are the builder. Move like it."

Chapter 8

NIL, AAU & Sneaker Politics — The Game Inside The Game

"If you don't understand the room you're in, you'll mistake the spotlight for safety — and the deal for love."

The New Era Of Basketball: Money Before Minutes

In the old days, you didn't see money in basketball until your name got called on draft night.

Now?

- 13-year-olds have brand deals.
- AAU programs fly private.
- Parents hire media teams before they hire tutors.
- Sneaker circuits scout kids like stocks.

It's not just about talent anymore.

It's about **exposure, narrative, politics,** and **who controls your story**.

This chapter will break down three systems shaping the future of basketball:

1. NIL (Name, Image, Likeness)

2. AAU Power Structures
3. Sneaker Circuits (Nike, Adidas, Under Armour)

Let's break the myths and teach you how to **move smart**.

SECTION 1

Nil — The Money Is Here. Now What?

What Is NIL?

NIL stands for **Name, Image, and Likeness** — your right as a student-athlete to **make money off your brand**.

Passed in July 2021, this NCAA policy lets high school and college athletes:

- Sign endorsement deals
- Start businesses
- Monetize social media
- Sell merch, host camps, and more

Who's Getting NIL Deals?

NIL deals aren't just for NBA-bound superstars. Here's a breakdown of the different types of players securing deals — and how they're doing it:

- **5-Star Recruits**
    - These top-tier high school or college players are earning $500K to $1 million+ from national brands, sneaker companies, and boosters.
    - Example: Endorsement deals from companies like Puma, Gatorade, or local sponsors tied to major college programs.
- **Mid-Level D1 College Players**

- Players who may not be viral stars but have strong local or regional followings.
- NIL earnings typically range from $10K to $75K per year, often from car dealerships, restaurants, apparel shops, or alumni connections.

- **Social Media Creators**
  - Athletes with large followings on TikTok, Instagram, or YouTube — even if they don't start on their team.
  - Many earn $1K to $5K per post or more just for sponsored content, product reviews, or lifestyle brand collaborations.

- **Elite AAU or High School Players**
  - Early buzz can lead to apparel deals, merch launches, or NIL partnerships while still in high school (depending on state laws).
  - Some players receive pre-college offers or brand seeding from sneaker companies.

Examples:

- **Mikey Williams**: Signed a multi-year sneaker deal with Puma before graduating high school.
- **Livvy Dunne** (gymnastics): Makes millions yearly from TikTok + NIL despite not being a household name in sports.

The Truth About NIL:

- **NIL is not just about being "famous."** It's about storytelling, content, and branding.
- If you're not building a presence, **you're invisible to the NIL economy.**
- Most athletes won't get million-dollar deals — but you can still earn **$10K–$50K+ annually** just by having a clear brand.

How To Win In The NIL Era

To take full advantage of NIL (Name, Image, and Likeness) opportunities, you have to be more than just a good athlete — you have to treat yourself like a brand. Here's how to win:

- **1. Clean Up Your Social Media**
    - Remove negativity, drama, or anything that could scare off sponsors.
    - Keep your profile professional, motivational, and focused on your journey.
- **2. Post Consistent Basketball Content**
    - Share your workouts, highlights, behind-the-scenes moments, and life as an athlete.
    - Let people connect with your story, not just your stats.
- **3. Engage with Local Brands and Businesses**
    - Reach out to barbershops, gyms, restaurants, or clothing stores in your area.
    - Offer to promote them in exchange for gear, food, or a small deal.
- **4. Tell a Unique Story**
    - NIL isn't always about being the best — it's about being different.
    - What makes you stand out? (Comeback story, faith, family, leadership, overcoming injury?)
- **5. Build a Small Personal Team**
    - Recruit a videographer, editor, or social media-savvy friend to help you stay consistent.
    - Even a two-person team can grow your brand faster than doing it all alone.

- **6. Learn the Rules in Your State or School**
    - Every state and school has different NIL policies.
    - Make sure you're following the compliance rules to avoid losing eligibility.

SECTION 2

AAU — The Empire Behind The Jerseys

What Is AAU?

AAU (Amateur Athletic Union) isn't just a league — it's a network.
A political machine.
A **scouting gateway**.

It connects players with:

- College coaches
- Sneaker reps
- Scouts and ranking services
- Videographers and media outlets

But **AAU isn't just about hoops — it's about hierarchy**.

The Truth About AAU Politics

AAU basketball is more than games and tournaments — it's a political machine. Who you play for and how you're promoted can matter more than how good you actually are. Here's what you need to know:

- **Your Team Matters More Than Your Stats**
    - Being on a popular or sponsored AAU team gives you more exposure, even if you're not the star.
    - A player averaging 10 points on a top EYBL team may get more offers than a player averaging 25 on a local squad.

- **Coaches Control Exposure**
    - Some AAU coaches won't send your highlights or talk to scouts unless you're "their guy."
    - Politics often decide who gets attention — not just talent.
- **Favoritism Is Real**
    - Some players get more minutes, better matchups, or more media simply because of who their parents know or what their reputation is.
- **Some Teams Are Built for Instagram, Not Development**
    - A few AAU programs focus more on clout and social media hype than actually preparing kids for the next level.
    - Watch out for teams that only post wins — not workouts, not training, not growth.

Example:
A 16-year-old on a top EYBL (Nike circuit) team can get more exposure than a 25 PPG high school star on a weak local team.

But...

- Politics can crush confidence
- Some coaches use players for clout
- Some programs chase sponsorships, not player growth

How to Survive AAU Without Getting Lost

- Pick a program that values **development and exposure** equally
- If your coach isn't promoting you, **promote yourself** (film, highlights, socials)
- Stay humble — but never be silent about your value

- Treat every tournament like an open job interview

SECTION 3

Sneaker Circuits — The Real Gatekeepers

The Three Giants:

- Nike EYBL
- Adidas 3SSB
- Under Armour Association

These circuits control:

- The top teams
- The top tournaments
- The most scouts
- The media coverage
- The player rankings

If you're not on the circuit, you're often out of sight — even if you're **better** than ranked players.

How Players Get on Sneaker Circuit Teams:

- Through AAU scouts, invites, and sponsorship alignment
- Top players get recruited by the teams
- Mid-tier players have to grind through open showcases and referrals

But beware:

- Politics run deep
- Favoritism exists
- Some coaches chase exposure for themselves, not players

Still Want In? Here's How to Play the Long Game

- Build your film and make it undeniable
- Train with players who are already in those circuits
- Go to open tryouts and camps

- Make noise locally — win MVPs, drop 30, stay in the gym
- Tag programs in your content (IG, Twitter, Hudl)

Spotlight Story

The Girl Who Got Dropped — And Built Her Own Team

Name: Kiana Ross
Hometown: Stone Mountain, GA
Dream: WNBA — or bust.

Kiana played on a high-level girls' Under Armour team. She worked hard. Put up numbers. Then one summer, **they cut her for a "bigger name" recruit.**

She was devastated.

Her mom told her: "We're not begging to belong. Let's build."

They created their own team. Just eight girls. Bought uniforms themselves. Entered local tournaments.
Started winning.
Then filming games.
Then Kiana started **documenting her journey** on TikTok and Instagram.

She caught the attention of mid-major schools.
Then got invited to a D1 elite camp.
She now plays on a full scholarship — and her story has **over 2 million views.**

Real Talk:
"I was tired of waiting for a seat at the table. So I grabbed a folding chair and started cooking."

Playbook Moment:
- Being dropped doesn't define you

- Exposure is not owned — it's earned and built
- The internet is your agent now — use it right

"If they won't call your name — make them see your work."

"Basketball isn't just played in gyms anymore. It's played in algorithms, reels, showcases, and stories."

"Build the game. Don't just play it."

Let's build.

Chapter 9 is where we **lay out the blueprint — 20+ real basketball-related careers**, all with $200K+ potential, each one detailed with:

- What it is
- How it pays
- How to get started
- Why it matters

Same professional tone. Same clear structure. Same fire.

Chapter 9

20+ Careers in Basketball That Pay — $200K and Beyond

"The game is bigger than the court. And your success can be bigger than the score."

The Dream Shift: From Player To Power

Let's be clear:

You don't need to play in the NBA to make **NBA-level money**.
You don't need to go D1 to build a D1-level brand.
You don't even need to make varsity to impact the game at the **highest levels**.

Basketball is a **multi-billion-dollar ecosystem**, and these roles prove it.

You just need to pick your lane — and commit to it like a championship run.

Let's break down **20+ real careers** that connect to the game and pay **$200,000+ or more** — depending on how hard you push and how smart you move.

1. Private Skills Trainer (Youth–Pro)

What They Do: Teach ball handling, footwork, shooting, IQ
Pay: $60–$200/hr | $100K–$400K/year
Start Here: Train a few local kids, film everything, post results, grow online
Why It Works: The best trainers build cult followings and get referrals nonstop.

2. NIL Agency Founder / Manager

What They Do: Handle sponsorships, contracts, and social strategy for athletes
Pay: 10–20% commission | $100K–$1M+
Start Here: Understand NIL rules, build your brand, sign 1–2 clients
Why It Works: Athletes need help navigating deals — and trust people who move smart.

3. AAU Program Director

What They Do: Organize teams, travel, tournaments, and player exposure
Pay: $75K–$300K+ depending on sponsorships and alumni impact
Start Here: Launch 1–2 teams, build a culture, create annual showcases
Why It Works: Parents will invest in development + access.

4. College Recruiting Analyst

What They Do: Scout players, track talent, run databases
Pay: $50K–$150K | top scouts land consulting roles
Start Here: Watch film, post rankings, start a Substack or blog
Why It Works: Coaches rely on trusted eyes to find the next wave.

5. YouTube Basketball Creator

What They Do: Break down games, create series, tell stories
Pay: Ads, sponsorships, digital products | $0–Unlimited
Start Here: Pick a niche: reactions, analysis, storytelling — post 2x/week
Why It Works: Consistent content turns followers into a business.

6. Social Media Manager (Team or Athlete)

What They Do: Run IG/TikTok/X content for athletes or programs
Pay: $60K–$200K+ (freelance or salaried)
Start Here: Do it free for one player, prove results, scale
Why It Works: Attention is currency. If you manage attention, you manage growth.

7. Basketball Podcast Host

What They Do: Interview players, coaches, analysts, trainers
Pay: Sponsorships + ad revenue | $0–$500K
Start Here: Get a mic, pick a lane, release weekly
Why It Works: Niche voices with strong consistency get loyal followings.

8. Gear/Apparel Brand Founder

What They Do: Sell gloves, hoodies, shooting sleeves, slogans
Pay: Unlimited | $0–$1M+
Start Here: Create one strong brand design, launch via Shopify, IG
Why It Works: If you speak culture, you can sell culture.

9. College Assistant Coach / Player Development

What They Do: Train, scout, and develop student-athletes
Pay: $50K–$200K+ depending on program level
Start Here: Start as a grad assistant or volunteer. Be irreplaceable.
Why It Works: Once you're in the college pipeline, loyalty = growth.

10. NBA or G-League Team Staff (Ops, Media, Strategy)

What They Do: Handle logistics, scouting, PR, film, player services
Pay: $70K–$250K+
Start Here: Intern, then outwork the room. Offer value constantly.
Why It Works: Pro teams need people who make everything move.

11. Videographer / Highlight Editor

What They Do: Film mixtapes, tournaments, training, IG clips
Pay: $100–$500/session | $80K–$200K+
Start Here: Edit on CapCut or Adobe Premiere, post clean, cinematic reels
Why It Works: Great visuals make good players look great — and they'll pay for it.

12. Camp Host / Showcase Organizer

What They Do: Create events that give players a platform
Pay: $10K–$150K+ per event depending on turnout/sponsorship
Start Here: Host a 30-player camp. Focus on value + media.
Why It Works: The exposure economy is booming — people pay to be seen.

13. Player Branding Consultant

What They Do: Build personal brands for rising athletes
Pay: $75K–$300K+ depending on clients
Start Here: Audit one athlete's brand and build their NIL kit
Why It Works: Players want to stand out — you show them how.

14. Strength and Conditioning Coach (Basketball Focused)

What They Do: Build agility, strength, injury prevention programs
Pay: $80K–$220K+
Start Here: Get certified (CSCS), train a few players, specialize

Why It Works: The best players trust their bodies to the best minds.

15. Sports Psychology / Mental Skills Coach

What They Do: Help athletes stay focused, confident, and resilient
Pay: $100K–$300K+
Start Here: Psych degree + sports specialization + testimonials
Why It Works: The mental game is now the X-factor — especially for elite athletes.

16. Photographer / Creative Director

What They Do: Shoot game days, portraits, edits, media day visuals
Pay: $75K–$250K+
Start Here: Build a portfolio at local gyms, tag everyone, deliver heat
Why It Works: Everyone wants to look like a pro — and will pay for it.

17. Agent / Contract Negotiator

What They Do: Represent pros in the NBA, G-League, or overseas
Pay: 3–10% of player salaries | $200K–$2M+
Start Here: Law or business degree + agency license + build rep
Why It Works: The right rep can change a player's career. Trust is everything.

18. Overseas Scout / International Liaison

What They Do: Help players sign contracts abroad
Pay: $60K–$200K+ (commission-based or agency salary)
Start Here: Learn international rules, contact Euro teams, build player portfolio
Why It Works: The U.S. isn't the only option. Smart scouts help talent find the right fit globally.

19. Tournament Manager (Circuit-Level)

What They Do: Oversee travel circuits, bracket builds, team relations
Pay: $80K–$200K+
Start Here: Work a regional event, network, get trusted by decision-makers
Why It Works: Good event managers run everything behind the curtain.

20. Basketball Curriculum Creator (Online Business)

What They Do: Sell shooting plans, drills, footwork programs
Pay: $0–Unlimited (digital product)
Start Here: Record drills, package them into an ebook or video series
Why It Works: Digital never sleeps. You can earn while you sleep.

Bonus Roles

These roles are often overlooked but can be just as lucrative and impactful in the basketball space:

- **Motivational Speaker (Basketball Focused)**
    - What They Do: Share personal stories, teach life lessons, and inspire athletes, schools, or corporate teams.
    - Estimated Pay: $1,000 to $10,000 per speech (more with demand, books, or viral reach)
- **Referee (High School, College, or Pro)**
    - What They Do: Officiate basketball games at various levels; high-level refs may also train others.
    - Estimated Pay: $40,000 to $250,000 per year (NBA refs earn the most)

- **Content Strategist (Basketball Brands or Athletes)**
    - What They Do: Build digital plans, manage messaging, and drive growth through social media, blogs, and visuals.
    - Estimated Pay: $70,000 to $200,000+ depending on brand and client size
- **Mobile App Developer (Basketball Tech)**
    - What They Do: Build apps for drills, highlights, stats, fantasy, and fan engagement.
    - Estimated Pay: Varies — potential is unlimited, especially with ownership or subscription-based platforms

Spotlight Story: The Ball Boy Who Became The Brand

Name: Desmond "D-Money" Taylor
Hometown: Columbus, Georgia
Dream: Wanted to hoop. Cut freshman year. Heart broken.

But he started designing flyers for team tryouts.
That turned into media day designs.
That turned into editing mixtapes for his friends.
Then trainers.
Then teams.
By 22, he launched **TaylorMade Graphics**, working with D1 athletes and NIL agencies.

- Averaging **$18K/month**
- Has his own studio
- Just signed a deal with a Nike-sponsored AAU team

Real Talk:
"I never made the team. But now the team calls me every week."

Playbook Moment:
- Your talent might be off the court — but it's just as valuable
- If you solve a need, you create a lane
- Build from what they overlook

"You don't have to play like a pro to get paid like one. Just think like one — and move with intention."

Chapter 10

Her Game Is Global — How Female Athletes Are Owning The Court And The Check

"She wasn't just built to play in the system. She was built to change it."

Why This Chapter Matters

Let's be real:
Female athletes grind just as hard as the boys.
Sometimes harder.
But they face:

- Fewer roster spots
- Less media coverage
- Lower average pay
- And more pressure to be perfect in every space — on the court and online

But here's the flip side:
Women's sports are exploding.
And the ones who know how to move smart?
They're building **brands**, **businesses**, and **blueprints** that last beyond the buzzer.

This chapter is for them.

The Numbers They Don't Tell You

Let's start with basketball:
- **WNBA Total Roster Spots:** Just **144** (12 teams × 12 players)
- **Average WNBA Salary:** Around **$130,000** (top stars earn $200K–$500K+ with bonuses & endorsements)
- **Overseas Pay:** Some WNBA players make **$500K–$1M overseas**, especially in Russia, Turkey, or China
- **NCAA Women's Basketball (All Divisions):** **~30,000 players**
- **Odds of Making the WNBA:** Less than 1% — similar to men's NBA odds, but with far fewer teams

What's Missing? Real Respect — And Real Game Plans

Female athletes have to deal with:
- Being judged on looks as much as talent
- Being underpaid, even when outperforming male counterparts
- Getting less coverage, less gear, and fewer investment dollars
- Getting told, "You should be thankful to just play"

But that's changing.
And the new wave of female athletes?
They're not asking for permission.

They're building brands, platforms, and checks — right now.

How Female Athletes Are Winning Off The Court

Here's how real women are stacking income, influence, and impact:

- **NIL Deals:** Women like Livvy Dunne (LSU Gymnastics) and Caitlin Clark (Iowa Basketball) are clearing **7 figures**
- **Merchandise:** Athletes are launching their own fashion lines, sports bras, and sneaker collabs
- **YouTube & TikTok:** Some female hoopers have built **six-figure media platforms** — showing workouts, vlogs, and reactions
- **International Leagues:** Players make more money overseas than in the U.S., and some double-dip in both
- **Training & Mentoring:** Female athletes are now training the next generation of girls through camps and mentorship programs

Ways Female Athletes Are Monetizing The Game

- **1. Personal Brand Building**
    - Using social media to showcase personality, not just performance
    - Platforms: IG, TikTok, YouTube
    - Focus: style, motivation, day-in-the-life, workouts
- **2. NIL Strategy**
    - Partnering with brands in fashion, wellness, fitness, or women-focused products
    - Ex: beauty partnerships, sneaker collabs, fitness products, skincare deals
- **3. Training & Mentorship**
    - Hosting clinics or camps for girls in middle school or high school

- o   Building a community around female empowerment + sports development
- **4. Podcasting & Media Creation**
    - o   Hosting interviews, sharing stories, talking real-life challenges
    - o   Creating platforms that give voice to underrepresented athletes
- **5. International Careers**
    - o   Signing overseas to earn more than WNBA salaries
    - o   Building a global brand while expanding cultural experience

Barriers They're Still Breaking

Let's tell the truth:

- Some schools still underfund girls' teams
- Some male coaches don't believe in investing in girls' sports
- Some fans still treat female athletes like a sideshow
- And many young women are still taught: "Be quiet, be pretty, be humble."

But here's the truth: **You can be loud.**
You can lead.
You can dominate.
And you can get paid doing it.

Spotlight Story: The Girl Who Said "Watch Me"

Name: Zahara Bell
Hometown: Savannah, Georgia
Dream: WNBA — then coaching. Then ownership.

Zahara was undersized.
She didn't go D1.
She didn't have a million followers.

But she built her platform slowly — sharing videos about leadership, injuries, pressure, and prayer.
She trained local girls on weekends.
Started a girls-only skills academy.
Launched a podcast with former college hoopers.

By age 25:

- She earned over **$100K+ in training and brand deals**
- Built a **3K+ email list** for her camp business
- Got hired by a prep school to lead girls' basketball operations
- Now mentoring high schoolers and helping parents navigate recruiting

Real Talk:
"They didn't want to let me in — so I just walked around and built my own gym."

Playbook Moment:

- There is no blueprint for women — so build one
- You are the brand
- Lead with authenticity, and the right people will find you

"She's not playing for respect — she's playing to build legacy."

"If no one hands you the keys, start your own engine."

"The era of silent excellence is over — speak up, cash in, lead loud."

Chapter 11

From The Sideline To The Stream — Fresh Ways To Make Money In Basketball

"Just because you're not on the roster doesn't mean you're not in the game. Money moves from every angle — especially from the ones no one sees coming."

The Lie: "If You Don't Play, You Don't Eat"

That mindset?
Outdated.

Basketball is a global, digital, and cultural machine — and the people eating the best are often nowhere near the court.

Today, fans don't just want stats.
They want stories.
They want style.
They want sound.
They want **access**.

And that's where the sideline comes in.

This chapter breaks down **underrated and overlooked** ways to turn basketball into **income, influence, and independence** — even if you never made the team.

Fresh Ways To Make Money From The Sideline

1. Storyteller for the Culture

- Start a YouTube or podcast series breaking down unknown hoop stories
- Cover neighborhood legends, underdog teams, motivational comeback stories
- Use Instagram Reels or TikTok to highlight moments that traditional media ignores
- Make money through sponsorships, ads, and affiliate links

Think: "The shop talk version of 30 for 30" — authentic, raw, community-based

2. Skill Session Plug

- You don't have to be the trainer — just the **organizer**
- Set up private sessions for local trainers, manage scheduling, collect payments
- Take a **cut per session** or charge monthly for admin & marketing
- Upsell with merch, video recaps, or parent-facing reports

You build the pipeline — trainers and parents just walk through it.

3. Social Media Game Manager

- Help young athletes or small AAU teams manage content
- Weekly plan: 1 highlight post, 1 quote, 1 recap video
- Charge per athlete or team: $200–$1,000/mo
- Perfect for college students, creatives, or parents with editing skills

Everyone wants to go viral — but no one wants to do the work. You step in.

4. Merch Drop Coordinator

- Partner with a local team or player to launch exclusive shirts or hoodies
- Run 1-month drops with 1–2 designs, take 40% of profits
- Market through local games, social media, or sneaker culture
- Scale by working with more teams or creating regional themes

Think: AAU x Fashion collab with real community roots.

5. Gym Plug / Practice Broker

- Find open gym space for teams or trainers who need it
- Negotiate the hourly rate, add a service fee for managing it
- You earn **without owning anything** — just through access

The person who controls the space controls the schedule — and the check.

6. Mic'd Up Moments Seller

- Offer players or coaches wearable mics during practice or camps
- Edit the funniest, rawest, most hype moments into social clips
- Post to YouTube, monetize traffic or sell branded video packages

The world loves authenticity. Capture it. Edit it. Sell it.

7. Digital Highlight Consultant

- Don't make the mixtapes — teach parents how to do it
- Sell a course, workshop, or 1:1 Zoom sessions
- Provide templates, editing apps, and filming strategies
- Once built, you can **sell this service at scale**

You're not an editor — you're the bridge that makes every parent a highlight creator.

8. Basketball Business Broker

- Connect trainers with sponsors
- Connect leagues with gyms
- Connect players with merch designers
- Charge a flat fee or percentage per deal

Be the middleman with a master plan. Relationships = revenue.

What All These Lanes Have In Common

- You don't need to hoop.
- You don't need to coach.
- You don't even need a big following.

You just need:

- **Value**
- **Consistency**
- **Execution**

Because the game doesn't only pay those who sweat.

It pays those who **solve problems**, **create access**, and **build behind the scenes**.

Spotlight Story: The Kid With The Iphone Hustle

Name: Malik St. James
Hometown: Jacksonville, FL
Background: Never made varsity. No real interest in coaching. Just loved being around the game.

Malik was always filming his boys' practices with an old iPhone. One day, he chopped up a 15-second clip, dropped a beat under it, and posted it.

It hit 20,000 views overnight.

So he kept going.

Now?

- Runs **"HoopCulture Media"**, filming raw mic'd up workouts, behind-the-scenes footage, and IG Reels for 10+ AAU programs
- Makes **$8,000–$12,000/month** off video packages, team media retainers, and content strategy consulting
- Just signed a brand deal with a sneaker store for exclusive sideline content

Real Talk:

"They laughed when I said I was just filming. Now they're paying me to post what they can't even create."

Playbook Moment:

- Start where you are
- Use what you have
- Build what they're too distracted to see

"You don't need a whistle to lead. You don't need a jersey to win. You just need a solution — and the heart to move first."

"The sideline isn't the end of the story. For some of us, it's where the business begins."

Chapter 12

Final Possession — Flip The Game, Don't Just Play It

"When you understand the rules, you can follow them. But when you master the game, you can change them."

You've Seen The Game. Now Own It.

You've made it through more than just a playbook — you've seen **the blueprint behind the scoreboard.**

You now understand:

- That the odds of going pro are slim — but the ways to **profit from the game** are endless
- That **value lives in the sidelines**, in the sneakers, in the content, and in the unseen
- That **girls and women in sports are rising fast**, building brands, leading lanes, and demanding equity
- That **your brand is your business** — and if you treat it like a joke, you'll be the punchline

This section taught the hustle beyond the hardwood.

It showed you how to turn the culture of basketball into currency. And most importantly: it reminded you that **you don't need access — you need action.**

Quick Recap: What You've Learned

- **The Numbers:**
    - Most don't make the league. But most don't need to — if they pivot wisely.

- **The Ecosystem:**
    - From high school to overseas, there's money in training, branding, content, nutrition, gear, mindset, storytelling, and more.

- **The Modern Hustle:**
    - The sideline is now a goldmine: social media, NIL consulting, merch, app building, podcasting, and personal branding.

- **The Female Takeover:**
    - Women athletes are leading — not just in sports, but in fashion, media, mentorship, and business.

- **The Compound Effect:**
    - Consistency beats hype. Small moves done daily become long-term wins.

- **The Gatekeeping Game:**
    - AAU politics, sneaker circuits, and old-school systems still exist — but now you know how to **navigate, outsmart, or create your own lane**.

- **The Sideline Hustle:**
    - We gave you fresh ideas: gym broker, merch plug, mic'd-up content creator, highlight consultant, media strategist, and more.

Spotlight Story: Rich Paul — The Man Who Crashed The Party And Bought The Table

Name: Rich Paul
Hometown: Cleveland, Ohio
Start: No college degree. No law background. Just hustle, loyalty, and vision.

In the early 2000s, Rich Paul was selling vintage jerseys out of his trunk.
That's how he met LeBron James.
They stayed close. Trusted each other.

Rich didn't take the traditional agent route. He didn't intern. He didn't get certified early.
He **studied the system** instead — and then outworked everybody in it.

He founded **Klutch Sports Group** and signed not just LeBron, but a **wave of top NBA players**:

- Anthony Davis
- Draymond Green
- Trae Young
- Zach LaVine
- And more

Then came the pushback.

In 2019, the NCAA tried to **ban agents without college degrees**. Everyone knew who that was aimed at.

They called it the **"Rich Paul Rule."**

He didn't fold.
He didn't apologize.

He **wrote an op-ed in The Athletic**, broke it down, and made it clear:

"Requiring a four-year degree excludes people who come from different backgrounds. I didn't go to college, but I knew my value — and I still do."

Today, Rich Paul is:

- Head of **Klutch Sports**
- Partnered with **United Talent Agency**
- One of the **most powerful figures in basketball**
- Worth over **$100 million**
- Engaged to **Adele** (yeah, that Adele)

Real Talk:
"I didn't break the system. I just refused to wait for it to invite me in."

Playbook Moment:

- Be loyal to your vision
- Build credibility through consistency
- When they try to block your door, build the next building

"You don't have to play for them to pay you."
"In every gym, every season, and every city — there's always more than one way to win."
"You are the brand. You are the business. You are the breakthrough."

Chapter 13

Diamonds And Data — Understanding The Baseball Pipeline

"The game rewards the patient, the precise, and the prepared. Know the system — or get benched by it."

Baseball Isn't Just A Game. It's A Journey.

No other major American sport stretches the path from childhood to pro as long as baseball.

From **Little League diamonds** to **minor league buses**, the route to Major League Baseball (MLB) is filled with:

- Years of training
- Late-night doubleheaders
- Injuries that don't go viral
- And dozens of stop signs before you ever touch a professional field

That's what makes this chapter crucial:

Before you swing for the fences, you better **study the field.**

The Baseball Funnel: From Little League To The Show

Here's a breakdown of how many players start and how few make it:

Little League / Youth Baseball

- Over **2.6 million kids** (ages 4–12) play in Little League annually
- Add travel ball and rec leagues, and youth participation jumps closer to **4 million**

High School Baseball (U.S.)

- Approximately **500,000 boys** play high school baseball each year
- Only about **7.5%** will go on to play at any level of college baseball

College Baseball

- Around **34,000 players** compete across NCAA Division I, II, III, NAIA, and JUCO
- Of those, only **about 9%** will be **drafted or signed** by a professional team

MLB Draft

- **Only 20 rounds** (as of 2021, down from 40 in previous years)
- That's roughly **600–650 players** drafted per year
- Most picks go to **college juniors/seniors or elite high school talent**

Minor Leagues (MiLB)

- Players start in Rookie ball or Low-A
- Climb to High-A → Double-A → Triple-A
- Only **10% of drafted players ever reach the Major Leagues**

MLB Roster

- **30 teams × 26 active players = 780 MLB spots**
- That includes **pitchers, catchers, infielders, and outfielders**

The Harsh Truth: The Grind Is Real

- **Average MLB career length:** just **2.7 years**
- **Most minor league players** earn **$20K–$30K per year**, with no guarantee of promotion
- **Injuries** (especially pitchers) are common:
    - Tommy John surgery (UCL reconstruction) has **become a norm** for many young arms
    - Common issues: rotator cuff tears, labrum damage, stress fractures, hip injuries

Even elite talent can **spend 6–8 years in the minors** before getting "the call"

Some never do.

Why Baseball Is So Hard To Navigate

- **No one path:** Some go from high school → MLB, others go college → minors → overseas → back again
- **Hard to get seen:** Without showcases, travel ball, or private trainers, most players are invisible
- **Extremely technical:** A .300 batting average means you fail 7 out of 10 times
- **It's a mental game:** Confidence is currency. Slumps break spirits fast.

And Yet... There's Still Big Money In Baseball

- MLB contracts are **fully guaranteed** (unlike NFL)
- Players like Shohei Ohtani, Mike Trout, and Aaron Judge are signing **$300M–$600M deals**

- Some **top agents, performance coaches,** and **media figures** in baseball are making **7 figures** — and **they never played a single inning**

Compound Truth: Most People Don't Look at the Map — Just the Mountaintop

That's why most players — and parents — get lost.

They only see:

"MLB or bust."

But they don't see:

- Player development
- Scouting
- Recruiting
- Performance analytics
- Rehab & return-to-play roles
- Brand building and NIL in college
- Latin America development pipelines
- Media and storytelling in the baseball ecosystem

Playbook Shift: Know Where You Stand — Then Move With Intent

Are you:

- A top-5% talent?
- A solid athlete who needs a different angle?
- A passionate baseball head who just wants to be in the game?

Each one has a path — but only if you know what's **really available.**

Spotlight Story: The Arm They Overlooked

Name: Jared Mendez
Hometown: Bakersfield, California
Position: Pitcher
Dream: Make it to the big leagues. No shortcuts. No excuses.

Jared wasn't a flame-thrower. He wasn't ranked.
He didn't have a personal trainer or private pitching lab.
But what did he have?
A dad who threw with him every morning at 6AM.
And a spiral notebook filled with every pitch location, every strikeout, every earned run he gave up since he was 11.

Jared walked on at a small JUCO in central California.
Coaches told him his velocity was too low.
So he studied mechanics. Learned breathing techniques. Mastered control.

By sophomore year:

- He threw **87 mph with precision**
- Was leading the state in **strikeouts-to-walks**
- And had created a **YouTube channel** breaking down "How to Pitch with Low Velocity and Win"

His videos gained traction — first 1,000 views, then 10,000.
A pitching coach from a mid-major D1 saw him and offered him a scholarship.

Jared transferred, kept documenting the process.
He never got drafted — but after graduation, was hired by that same coach to be a **player development assistant**.

Now he:

- Works with over **50 pitchers** across D1, JUCO, and high school
- Built a side business selling pitch tracking spreadsheets and mental game eBooks
- Speaks at baseball coaching clinics nationwide
- Made **$112,000 last year** — never throwing 90 mph in his life

Real Talk:
"I wasn't built for ESPN. I was built to help the kids who never got filmed."

Playbook Moment:
- Use what you have
- Document your journey
- Turn your obstacle into an operating system

"You don't have to be drafted to be dangerous. You just need the vision to see what others overlook — and the guts to act on it."

Chapter 14

20+ Baseball Careers That Pay — $200K And Beyond

"In a game where failure is part of the rhythm, the ones who win are the ones who see the field differently."

You Don't Need A Bat To Get Paid

Baseball is tradition. It's storytelling. It's statistics. It's science. And behind every swing, pitch, and highlight… there's a **system of workers**, leaders, and creators making **big money** off the game.

This chapter is about them.

We're breaking down **over 20 real baseball-related careers** that can earn you **$200,000+ per year** — whether you're a former player, a data head, a strategist, or a creative.

20+ Baseball Careers That Pay

1. Player Development Director

- Oversees athlete progress and training plans in pro, college, or youth systems
- **Pay:** $90K to $250K+

2. Baseball Agent

- Represents players, negotiates contracts, secures brand deals
- **Pay:** Commission-based — top agents earn $500K to multi-millions annually

3. Minor League Organization Owner

- Buys into or builds small team franchises, manages operations and growth
- **Pay:** Depends on location, revenue streams — some owners clear $300K+

4. MLB Scout (Domestic or International)

- Evaluates talent at high school, college, or international levels
- **Pay:** $80K to $200K+ (senior scouts earn more)

5. College Baseball Recruiting Coordinator

- Leads recruiting for NCAA programs — builds team rosters
- **Pay:** $60K to $150K+

6. Pitching/Batting Specialist (Private Coach)

- Works with players 1-on-1 or in small groups on technique
- **Pay:** $100/hour to $250K+/year depending on client base

7. Baseball Performance Analyst (Data & Tech)

- Breaks down spin rate, bat speed, biomechanics, and more
- **Pay:** $90K to $220K+

8. Baseball Content Creator (YouTube, IG, TikTok)

- Creates baseball education, reviews, interviews, commentary
- **Pay:** Unlimited — $5K to $50K+/month through ads, sponsors, digital products

9. Tournament Director (Youth Travel Ball)

- Hosts weekend showcases and events for AAU-style travel teams

- **Pay:** $10K to $100K+ per event

10. Baseball Brand Owner (Apparel/Equipment)

- Sells gloves, shirts, bats, sleeves, or niche baseball gear
- **Pay:** Unlimited — depends on brand strength

11. Stadium Event Manager (Pro or College)

- Manages game day operations, ticketing, and logistics
- **Pay:** $75K to $200K+

12. NIL Brand Consultant (for College Athletes)

- Helps players monetize their brand legally
- **Pay:** $100K to $400K+

13. Videographer/Editor (Highlight + Recruiting Tapes)

- Works with players or teams to create pro-level footage
- **Pay:** $200–$1,000 per project | $75K to $150K+/year

14. Mental Skills Coach

- Helps athletes with focus, pressure, and recovery from slumps
- **Pay:** $80K to $250K+

15. Baseball App Developer

- Creates scorekeeping tools, scouting platforms, fan apps
- **Pay:** Unlimited — depending on user base and business model

16. International Player Liaison

- Works with Latin American or Asian athletes adjusting to U.S. systems
- **Pay:** $70K to $180K+

17. Athletic Trainer or Rehab Specialist

- Prevents or rehabs injuries; common in elbow, shoulder, hamstring
- **Pay:** $90K to $200K+

18. Gear Rep (Gloves, Bats, Uniforms)

- Works for major brands placing product with teams
- **Pay:** $70K to $180K+ with bonuses

19. Umpire (MLB or Minor League)

- Calls games at the highest level
- **Pay:** $120K to $300K+ (MLB level)

20. Sports Lawyer (Contracts + Arbitration)

- Handles legal work behind trades, contracts, endorsements
- **Pay:** $150K to $500K+

Real Opportunities. Real Strategy. No Excuses.

If you love the game — but the roster didn't call your name — it doesn't mean the door is closed.
It means it's time to walk into a **different room**.

Some of the most powerful people in baseball never had a walk-up song. But they know how to run the business.

Spotlight Story: The Guy With The Clipboard And The Code

Name: Andre Holloway
Hometown: Houston, Texas
Background: Played outfield in high school. D2 walk-on. Loved the game, but the bat wasn't elite.

Andre majored in data science. While riding the bench, he started building a software tool that tracked pitch sequences and swing tendencies.

Coaches laughed at first.
Two years later, an MLB scouting department bought a **beta license**.

Now?

- Andre runs **ProMetrics Baseball**, a player analysis software used by 7 college programs and 3 minor league systems

- Built a **$300K+/year tech business**
- Sits in meetings with general managers and trainers — wearing sneakers, not cleats

Real Talk:
"They told me I wasn't fast enough. Turns out, I just had to see the game differently."

Playbook Moment:

- Every game needs thinkers, builders, and systems
- Don't chase highlight reels — chase blind spots
- The smarter you move, the more the game needs you

"If the field doesn't fit your gift, step into the front office and change the script."

"Real power isn't earned in batting cages — it's built in back rooms, brainstorms, and belief."

Chapter 15

Start Where You Are — What You Can Do, What It Costs, And When To Begin

"The earlier you build the habit of creating value, the faster the game starts paying you back."

Why This Chapter Matters

A lot of people think you need:

- Big money
- A viral moment
- Or a perfect connection

To start making money around baseball.

You don't.

What you actually need is:

- A clear idea
- A small plan
- And the courage to start simple

Let's break it down into **real moves**, **start-up budgets**, and **the right age to begin** — so there are **no excuses** left on the field.

1. Start a Training Side Hustle
What You Can Do:
Offer private fielding, hitting, pitching, or conditioning sessions to younger players
Age You Can Start:
15+ (as long as you have skills and can lead kids)
What You Need:
- Glove, cones, a bat, a few drills
- Social media page to post availability
- Testimonials or before/after videos to show results

Budget to Start:
$0 to $150
(If you already have gear, you're set. Just start with 1 kid.)
Upside:
$25–$50 per session to start
Can grow to $100–$200/hour with experience

2. Launch a Highlight Edit Service
What You Can Do:
Edit recruiting footage, hype reels, or game recaps for high school and travel players
Age You Can Start:
13+ with a phone or laptop
What You Need:
- Free editing apps (CapCut, iMovie, InShot, Canva, or Adobe Rush)
- Music library (royalty-free or from TikTok trends)
- Sample video and pricing

Budget to Start:
$0 to $100
(Optional: Pay for premium editing apps or storage space)
Upside:
Charge $50 to $300 per reel
Can scale to monthly content packages

3. Build A Personal Brand Page (Player Or Entrepreneur)
What You Can Do:
Post workouts, game recaps, tips, or educational content
Age You Can Start:
Any age — but best at 12+ if you can stay consistent
What You Need:
- A clear message (are you teaching, documenting, or motivating?)
- A phone
- 2–3 posts per week
- Hashtags, music, and consistency

Budget to Start:
$0 to $50
(Optional: Invest in Canva Pro or a ring light)
Upside:
Build followers → attract NIL deals, sponsors, clients, or speaking gigs

4. Start a Mini Merch Brand (Baseball-Focused)

What You Can Do:
Sell baseball-themed hoodies, gloves, slogans, or gear

Age You Can Start:
13+ with a parent's help for payments

What You Need:

- Design platform (Canva or Adobe)
- Print-on-demand site (like Printful, Teespring, or Shopify)
- Logo, 2–3 designs, and marketing content

Budget to Start:
$0 to $200
(Shopify costs $39/month; Canva $13/month)

Upside:
Can earn hundreds to thousands per drop
Also builds brand recognition in your local baseball scene

5. Host a Pop-Up Skills Camp or Clinic

What You Can Do:
Invite local kids (ages 8–13) to a 1-day hitting or defense camp

Age You Can Start:
16+ (responsible high schoolers can partner with coaches or parks)

What You Need:

- Field access (school or park)
- Flyer
- 2–3 drills and structure
- Helpers (friends or teammates)
- Registration system (Google Form + Cash App)

Budget to Start:
$50 to $200
(For flyers, water, cones, and promo)

Upside:
Charge $20 to $50 per player
Host 20 players = $400 to $1,000+ day

6. Become a Game-Day Content Creator

What You Can Do:
Film mic'd-up warmups, funny dugout moments, or game recaps for travel teams

Age You Can Start:
14+ with basic editing and confidence

What You Need:

- Phone + tripod

- Voice-over or music
- Editing skills (CapCut, TikTok, iMovie)

Budget to Start:
$0 to $100
(Tripod + premium app access if needed)

Upside:
Teams may pay $100–$300 per weekend
You can also monetize your own content channel

7. Baseball Info Plug / Recruit Helper

What You Can Do:
Research camps, JUCOs, D2s, or advisors for overlooked players and help families plan

Age You Can Start:
17+ (need maturity and research skills)

What You Need:
- Spreadsheet
- Basic knowledge of eligibility, showcases, and timelines
- Clear email communication and trusted referrals

Budget to Start:
$0 to $50
(Optional: website or booking tool)

Upside:
Charge $50–$150 for sessions
Create a PDF or course to sell for passive income

The Truth: Most People Don't Get Paid Because They Never Start

You don't need a major league scout to find you.
You need to **act on the small tools in your hand** right now.

You already have:
- A phone
- Knowledge
- Social media
- A few connections
- A story
- A skill

The only thing you might be missing is **execution**.

Spotlight Story: The Kid With The Drill Bag

Name: Cam Reynolds
Hometown: Louisville, KY
Age Started: 16

Cam was a decent player — not a standout. But he was obsessed with footwork drills, glove angles, and throwing mechanics.

So he started helping his little cousin after school.

Then a neighbor asked.

Then two teammates' siblings.

Cam put together a bag with cones, a bucket of balls, and an Instagram page.

By senior year:
- He had 12 kids training with him weekly
- Hosted a $25 Saturday clinic every month
- Made **$7,000 his last year of high school**
- And built a **3K+ follower IG** that led to brand deals and speaking at a youth convention

Real Talk:
"I never hit a walk-off. But I helped 10 other kids feel like they did."

Playbook Moment:

- Simple drills turned into income
- Free reps turned into paying clients
- Small steps built something big

"Start where you are. Use what you have. Keep showing up — and the game will start paying you back."

"If you wait for the opportunity to be perfect, you'll miss the whole season."

Chapter 16

The Baseball Revenue Map — How The Game Pays If You Know Where To Stand

"The game doesn't just reward the elite. It rewards the informed."

The Truth: Baseball Is Quiet Money

You don't always see it trending.

But baseball moves **billions** every year.
From stadiums to scorecards.
From NIL deals to overseas leagues.
From merch to media.

Most people think:

"Only the MLB players get rich."

But the reality is:

Everyone from the trainer to the bat designer to the podcast host is getting paid — if they know how to play their position.

Let's Look At The Numbers

MLB Revenue (2023):

- Total League Revenue: **$11.6 billion**
- Average Team Value: **$2.32 billion**
- Most Valuable Team: **New York Yankees ($7.1 billion)**
- Top Player Salaries:
    - Shohei Ohtani: $700M deal (w/ deferrals)
    - Aaron Judge: $360M
    - Bryce Harper: $330M

College Baseball: What's The Opportunity?

Once you get to the college level — D1, D2, NAIA, or JUCO — several doors open:

1. NIL (Name, Image, Likeness) Money

- Players can earn by promoting brands, doing appearances, or selling merch
- Top D1 players: **$50K–$250K+** (especially with social media presence)
- Mid-level players: **$5K–$25K** via local brands or apparel deals

You don't need to be famous — just valuable to a niche.

2. Scholarship Savings = Earnings

- D1 schools offer partial scholarships (up to 11.7 full rides across 30+ players)
- JUCOs and D2s often stack aid through grants, housing, or books
- If a scholarship saves you **$20K–$30K/year**, that's **money kept in your pocket**

3. Summer Leagues & Exposure

- Cape Cod League, Northwoods, and others draw scouts and sponsorships
- Some offer stipends, housing, and meal money (around **$2,000–$5,000/summer**)
- Connections made here often lead to **draft invites or pro tryouts**

Minor Leagues (MiLB): The Hustle Phase

- Rookie League: **$20K–$25K/year**
- Low-A to Double-A: **$26K–$40K/year**
- Triple-A: Up to **$50K–$60K/year**, some bonuses

Most players live **month-to-month** unless they get a **signing bonus** (which can range from $10K to $8M depending on draft round)

But here's the key:

- Even if you never make MLB, just being **in the pro system** gives you leverage:
    - Camps
    - Coaching
    - Branding
    - Media
    - International offers

International & Overseas Baseball: The Hidden Goldmine

Japan (NPB):

- Top salaries: **$500K to $5M**
- Average: **$300K–$1M**
- Includes housing, travel, cultural perks

South Korea (KBO):

- Foreign player salaries: **$300K–$1M**
- More relaxed playing environment

- Strong fan base, opportunities to extend career

Latin America (Winter Leagues):

- Less money, but:
  - **Pays well short-term**
  - Offers exposure
  - Helps build off-season income streams (up to $20K–$80K per stint)

Coaching & Development: The Underrated Lane

High School Head Coach:

- $60K–$120K (depending on school + teaching role)
- Camps and private sessions = extra $20K–$50K+

College Assistant Coach:

- D1: $50K–$150K+
- Some assistants with hitting/pitching specializations earn $200K+

Pro Staff (Player Development, Scouting):

- $70K to $300K depending on level, experience, and specialty

The Media & Tech Side Of Baseball

The world of baseball analytics, storytelling, and content has exploded:

- **Statcast / Baseball Savant Analysts**: $80K–$150K+
- **Podcast Hosts (niche baseball commentary)**: Unlimited via ads, merch, subs
- **YouTube Creators (reactions, gear reviews, breakdowns)**: $1K–$50K/month

- **App Developers (training tech, scorekeeping)**: Can reach 6–7 figures if scaled

The Real Lesson: Don't Just Chase One Position. Know The Whole Field.

Too many people only aim for **shortstop or centerfield**.
But there's real power (and money) in knowing **every base of the business**.

You could:

- Play in college
- Coach part-time
- Run social media for a team
- Drop a podcast
- Host clinics
- Train kids
- Design baseball merch
- Build swing tech

One talent multiplies when you understand the system.

Spotlight Story: The Bench Player Who Became A Brand

Name: Devonte Reece
Hometown: Atlanta, GA
College: Played two years at an HBCU. Utility player. Great glove. Didn't start much.

Devonte loved baseball. But more than that — he loved the culture around it.

While riding the bench, he launched a clothing line called **"Slide Culture."**
Started with one hoodie:

"Practice Hard. Slide Better."

He wore it. His teammates wanted one. Then a rival team asked.

By year two:

- He was making **$5K/month online**
- Started filming behind-the-scenes HBCU baseball life
- Got an NIL partnership with a glove company
- Graduated, then signed as a **consultant for a D2 recruiting service** helping underserved players tell their story

Real Talk:
"I never made the starting lineup. But I made my name mean something."

Playbook Moment:

- Use what's in your locker
- Turn what's missing into what's marketable
- Your sideline can become your signature

"The money in baseball isn't just on the mound. It's in the margins, the media, the merch — and the mindsets bold enough to create."

"Don't just play the game. Learn how it flows — and follow the money."

Chapter 17

Diamonds & Deposits — How Softball Pays From College To Sunday League

"Softball doesn't end after college. It transforms. And those who keep showing up — keep stacking wins."

Softball = Community + Hustle

Unlike baseball, softball doesn't have a multi-billion-dollar pro league (yet).
But don't get it twisted — the money is **absolutely there**.

You just have to know:

- Where to look
- Who to serve
- How to build it from the dirt up

Whether you're playing D1, coaching travel ball, or hitting bombs in Sunday pickup — you can **turn your love for the game into real revenue.**

1. College-Level Softball: Where The Doors Open

NIL (Name, Image, Likeness)

- Female athletes in softball are killing it with social media + storytelling
- Top D1 players are landing **$5K–$200K+** in NIL deals (with beauty, wellness, apparel, or sports brands)

What You Can Do:

- Grow your IG, TikTok, or YouTube by posting training, team life, tips, and personality
- Build a brand around your journey — not just your stats
- Offer shoutouts, brand promotions, or custom merch

Age You Can Start:
16+ (once you hit college or even high-level travel ball)

Running Camps & Clinics (Weekend or Summer)

- College players can host hitting or fielding sessions during breaks
- Partner with local youth leagues or parks

Startup Budget:
$100–$300 (for flyers, cones, and water)
Revenue: $25–$100/player
20 kids = $500–$2,000+ weekend

Skill Coaching (1-on-1 or Small Groups)

- Work with younger girls who want to make JV/varsity or travel ball
- Fielding, catching, pitching, or hitting

Pay Rate:
$25–$100/hour
Startup Cost: Equipment you already own

Content Creator (Softball Focus)

- Breakdowns, gear reviews, pitching mechanics, mindset
- Add humor, vlogs, or mic'd-up moments

Platforms:
TikTok, IG, YouTube
Monetization: Ads, sponsors, affiliate links
Potential: $500–$5,000+/month if you stay consistent

2. Post-College & Long-Term Plays

Become a Travel Ball Coach or Director

- Start your own 12U/14U/16U program
- Charge monthly or seasonal fees
- Create an elite culture of development + exposure

Income Potential:
$10K–$50K+ annually (more if you run multiple teams or tournaments)

Host Local Tournaments or Showcase Events

- Rent a park, bring in 8–12 teams, charge entry + vendors
- Use media and highlight coverage to grow brand

Startup Budget:
$500–$2,000
Revenue: $5K–$25K per event (depending on sponsors + turnout)

Start a Softball Gear Brand or Merch Line

- Slogans, gloves, visors, batting gloves, shirts
- "Dirt Don't Lie," "Riseball Royalty," or city/team pride themes

Use platforms like:
Shopify, Printful, Teespring
Startup Cost: $0–$200
Upside: Passive income + brand-building

Work in College Recruiting or Consulting

- Help families understand scholarships, camps, videos, and timelines

- Offer one-on-one sessions, video reviews, or PDF guides

Potential Pay:
$50–$300/session

Great side hustle for former college players

Become a Umpire or Tournament Official

- Weekend gigs at youth leagues or tournaments
- Training provided by local associations

Pay Range:
$25–$75/game
Double-headers = $150+ weekends = $300–$600

3. Sunday League / Co-Ed Softball: Fun Meets Hustle

There's a whole economy built around **adult pickup softball** — and it's growing:

Sell Custom Team Jerseys or Hats

- Teams want drip. Create designs, team names, or heat-pressed slogans

Startup Cost:
$100–$250 (samples + vendor site)
Charge: $20–$40 per shirt
20 players = $800+

Create a Local League / Host Monthly Games

- Round up 4–6 teams, charge a small fee, get a DJ or food truck
- Create a vibe — not just a game

Startup Cost:
$300–$800
Revenue: $2K–$5K per event + future loyalty

Offer Game-Day Photography or Video Recaps

- Post highlights, slow-mo hits, or dugout hype reels

- Upsell players with personal edits

Startup Cost:
Phone or camera
Revenue: $100–$500/event

Start a Softball Podcast or YouTube Series

- Focus on the lifestyle: gear talk, mic'd-up games, team dynamics, female athlete empowerment

Earnings:
$0–$10K/month depending on views and sponsors

The Real: Softball Isn't Just A Phase — It's A Platform

Even if you don't go pro, you can go **profitable**.

Softball builds:

- Confidence
- Leadership
- Skill
- Content
- Community

And **community = commerce** when you serve it with authenticity.

Spotlight Story: The Park Queen Of Sunday Leagues

Name: Tameka Jones
Hometown: Detroit, MI
Background: Played JUCO ball, became a social worker. Still had love for the game.

She started a Sunday women's league called **Dirt Divas** — just 6 teams at first.
Made jerseys, hosted picnics, posted game recaps.
Brought in vendors. Local DJ. A drone guy.

Now?

- Runs 3 seasonal leagues
- Sells custom merch
- Hosts an annual **All-Star Co-Ed BBQ tournament**
- Makes **$25K+ per year** off something she started "just for fun"

Real Talk:
"This wasn't supposed to be a business. But when you build something with love, the money shows up too."

Playbook Moment:

- Start small
- Build your team
- Don't play small ball with your passion

"Softball doesn't end when the season does. It evolves. And if you treat it like a playground and a platform — it will bless you like both."

Chapter 18

Play On Purpose — Turning Passion Into Payment

"If the game lives in your heart, it can live on your terms. You just need vision, value, and the guts to move."

Let's Be Clear: You Don't Have To Go Pro To Win

If you've made it this far, you already know:

- The odds of going D1 or pro are slim
- Injuries, politics, and timing can change everything
- Talent is not always enough

But here's what's **always true**:

The game will pay those who understand how it flows.

You can't just show up.
You have to study.
You have to strategize.
You have to create lanes when the door doesn't open.

This Blueprint Showed You How

You now know:

- How football pays beyond touchdowns — through training, gear, media, coaching, and culture
- How basketball moves money through NIL, AAU, merch, mixtapes, podcasts, and development
- How baseball stacks revenue in colleges, minor leagues, tech, tournaments, scouting, and content
- How softball can fund your future — from college clinics to Sunday league empires
- How anyone — player, coach, creative, or fan — can find a lane if they lead with purpose and hustle

What Do All the Winners Have in Common?

Whether it was:

- Inky Johnson
- Rich Paul
- Andre the data guy
- Cam the drill bag kid
- Zahara the podcast queen
- Tameka from the park
- Or the Sunday league legend with a jersey hustle

They all did this:

1. They Started Small
They didn't wait for permission.
 They used what they had — and made it enough.

2. They Told Their Story
They didn't need a viral moment.
 They showed up with consistency.
 They let people feel the love behind the work.

3. They Added Value
To parents.
 To players.

To coaches.
To their own communities.

They solved real problems — and people paid for solutions.

4. They Stayed Authentic
No gimmicks. No pretending.
Just love for the game + smart execution.

So What's Next? Your Playbook Moves

If you're a player:

- Start building your brand.
- Teach what you know.
- Use your journey to inspire, mentor, and create.

If you're a parent:

- Support the whole game, not just the dream
- Invest in development, education, and storytelling
- Encourage creative lanes early

If you're a creative:

- Film it. Edit it. Design it. Sell it.
- The culture always needs content — own your role.

If you're a coach or organizer:

- Create events, run camps, mentor kids
- The structure you build becomes someone else's foundation

If you just love sports:

- That's enough.
- You can write, teach, film, talk, lead, sell, train, or design your way into this world.

Spotlight: The One Who Started This Book

This book didn't come from theory.
 It came from watching a generation chase one path — while sleeping on 20 others.

From seeing kids give up too soon because they didn't know what was really possible.

From understanding that the streets, the system, and the stats weren't built for our survival.

But **information is freedom**.

And the moment you realize your love for the game is a **currency** — not a limitation —
is the moment you stop waiting and start **building**.

Real Talk:
"You can make your passion your paycheck. But you gotta clock in."

"The dream isn't dead. It just got wider. Now it has cameras, clinics, merch, training bags, inboxes, media passes, booking forms, and blueprints."

"You don't have to go viral — you just have to go valuable."

"Play the game. Then own the game. Then pass it on."

Chapter 19

Quiet Power — The Real Game Of Golf

"Golf doesn't shout. It teaches. It pays those who master the stillness — and understand the system."

Let's Start With The Truth: Golf Is A Business With A Ball

It's not just a country club pastime.
It's not just for retirees or trust fund babies.

Golf is:

- A **$102 billion** global industry
- One of the only sports where athletes **can earn well into their 40s and 50s**
- A career **with no draft, no height requirement, no shot clock**
- And more importantly: a space where **networking, mental discipline, and long-game strategy** are built into the culture

The Golf Funnel: From Tee To Tour

Here's a breakdown of how the journey works — and how rare it is to go all the way.

Youth Golf (Ages 5–12):

- Over **3 million junior golfers** in the U.S.
- Most enter through:
    - The First Tee program
    - Local tournaments (U.S. Kids, PGA Junior League)
    - Private coaching
    - Community clubs

High School Golf:

- Roughly **220,000 boys and girls** play high school golf nationwide
- Most are self-funded: parents cover travel, gear, and entry fees
- College recruiters typically scout at **AJGA**, **Hurricane Tour**, or **state championships**

College Golf:

- **NCAA D1, D2, D3, NAIA, and JUCO** offer golf scholarships
- About **1.9% of high school golfers** make it to NCAA D1
- Only **0.6%** of college golfers will turn pro

The road to college alone is expensive — often **$10K–$25K per year** just to compete at the elite junior level

Turning Pro: The Reality Check

Unlike team sports, **golf has no draft**.
 You have to **earn your way up** through performance, persistence, and funding.

Step 1: Mini Tours & Q School

- Costly process — includes travel, caddies, tournament fees
- **$500–$1,200+ per event**, often with no prize if you don't make the cut
- Players need **$40K–$80K/year** just to chase the dream

Step 2: Korn Ferry Tour (Development League for PGA)

- Mid-level pros
- Top finishers each year can earn PGA Tour cards
- Still expensive: only top 30–50 players earn **$100K+**

Step 3: PGA Tour (U.S. Pro Circuit)

- **Top 125 players** keep their tour cards annually
- Prize money is massive —
  - Winners often take home **$1.5M–$3M per tournament**
  - Even 10th–20th finishers can earn **$200K–$500K+**

LIV Golf & International Tours

- LIV is backed by Saudi investment: signing bonuses in **tens of millions**
- Europe, Asia, South Africa also offer tour routes — many players build careers overseas

Setbacks In Golf: What They Don't Always Say

- **Expense:** It's one of the most expensive sports to pursue
- **Access:** Many young players — especially in urban or under-resourced communities — never touch a real course
- **Visibility:** Few inner-city or minority players get early exposure
- **Pressure:** It's one of the most mentally taxing sports — no teammates to fall back on
- **Burnout:** Starting too young without fun leads to dropouts in late teens

So Why Bother? Because The Wins Are Long-Term

- Golf teaches emotional control, financial discipline, patience

- A pro career can last **20+ years**
- Even college golfers or amateurs can:
    - Start brands
    - Coach or teach
    - Host clinics
    - Build real relationships with CEOs, athletes, and influencers
    - And use golf to **network into industries like law, finance, tech, or entertainment**

Spotlight Story: The Caddie Who Became A Contender

Name: Willie Mack III
Hometown: Flint, Michigan
Background: Slept in his car. Carried bags. Never lost his swing.

Willie didn't grow up with a country club membership.
He grew up with **grit**.

His dream was the PGA Tour — but he didn't have the money to chase it the way others did.
So he did what he had to:

- Lived out of his car at golf courses
- Took every free round he could get
- Entered mini-tours when he had enough to cover the fee
- Caddied and taught lessons to fund the next shot

At one point, he was winning events but **couldn't afford gas to get to the next one.**
Still, he kept showing up. Kept grinding.

Then in 2021, everything changed:

- He earned a sponsor's exemption into the **Farmers Insurance Open** (his PGA Tour debut)

- He later won the **Advocates Pro Golf Association (APGA) Tour Championship**
- Built a reputation as one of the most **resilient, talented, and humble golfers in the system**
- Now mentoring and opening doors for **Black youth and overlooked talent in golf**

Real Talk:
"I never wanted to be famous. I just wanted a shot. And when you live in your car, every shot matters."

Playbook Moment:

- Sometimes your hustle is louder than your swing
- Where you start doesn't limit where you finish
- If you keep showing up, the door can't ignore you forever

"I went from the parking lot to the leaderboard. Not because of luck — but because I refused to quit swinging."

Chapter 20

Green On The Greens — How Golf Pays When You Play It Smart

"In golf, the money isn't just in the swing — it's in the setup."

The Myth: Only Pros Get Paid In Golf

Let's break that now.
Because the truth is: **the most consistent money in golf is made by the ones who know how to teach, host, brand, and build around the game**.

You don't have to drive 300 yards.
You don't have to wear a green jacket.
You just have to know how to move in the ecosystem.

This chapter shows you **how to turn the course into cash** — no tour card required.

1. Golf Coach or Private Instructor

What You Do:
- Teach swing mechanics, short game, putting, or mental focus

- Work with kids, high schoolers, adults, beginners, or pros

Start-Up Cost:

- $500–$2,000 (for a launch monitor, club set, and booking site)
- Use driving ranges or mobile apps if you're starting lean

Pay:
- $50–$200/hour
- Some elite coaches earn **$100K–$500K+ per year**

Who Can Start:
- Former players, college athletes, or anyone with deep technical knowledge

2. Youth Golf Camp or Clinic Organizer

What You Do:

- Host 1–2 day skills camps at local courses or parks
- Serve kids age 7–17 who want to learn basics or prep for competition

Startup Budget:

- $250–$1,000 for flyers, snacks, insurance, and guest coaches

Revenue Potential:

- 20 kids × $75 = $1,500
- Multiple sessions = $5K–$15K summer hustle

Best For:

- College golfers, trainers, park program directors, or sports entrepreneurs

3. Golf Content Creator

What You Do:

- Post tutorials, tips, club reviews, course vlogs, mic'd up range sessions

- Create "lifestyle" content (funny, stylish, relatable)

Tools:

- Phone + tripod + CapCut or iMovie to start
- Optional: drone or GoPro

Monetization:

- YouTube ads
- TikTok creator fund
- Brand sponsors (golf gear, courses, golfwear)
- Affiliate links (Amazon, Golf Galaxy, etc.)

Pay Potential:

- Side hustle: $500–$3,000/mo
- Full-time: $10K–$50K+/mo (with brand growth)

4. Tournament Director / League Builder

What You Do:

- Host community scrambles, city tournaments, or club-level competitions
- Create a vibe: prizes, food, music, culture, and community

Startup Budget:

- $1,000–$5,000 (course rental, promo, food, trophies)

Revenue:

- $5K–$25K/event (through entry fees, vendors, and sponsors)

Ideal For:

- Creators, coaches, brand builders, or former players

5. Golf Brand Founder (Apparel or Gear)

What You Do:

- Sell polos, visors, gloves, hats, tees, or golf bags with your style/message

Startup Tools:

- Shopify + Printful or Teespring
- Design using Canva or Adobe

Cost to Launch:

- $0–$250 (no inventory needed if print-on-demand)

Profit Potential:

- Niche brands can make $1K–$10K/month
- Premium lines can scale to 6–7 figures

6. Mental Skills Coach or Confidence Strategist

What You Do:

- Help golfers stay focused, manage nerves, visualize success
- Often paired with elite juniors or college players

Requires:

- Experience + psychology/sports training
- You can also create online products (ebooks, journals, video courses)

Pay:

- $100–$300/hour
- Passive sales can reach $5K+/mo

7. Golf Social Media Manager (for Players or Courses)

What You Do:

- Run content, branding, or promo pages for local pros, influencers, or country clubs
- Film reels, post schedules, promote tournaments

Startup Cost:

- Free apps + Wi-Fi + content plan

Pay:
- $300–$2,000/month per client
- Perfect for teens, students, creatives

8. Golf Fitness Specialist

What You Do:
- Help players increase swing speed, core strength, flexibility, and injury prevention
- Create plans for youth, college, or adults

Certifications Help:
- TPI (Titleist Performance Institute) is the gold standard

Pay:
- $75–$150/hr
- Online training = $1K–$10K+/month

9. Corporate Golf Event Planner

What You Do:
- Plan charity tournaments, networking scrambles, or company golf outings
- Coordinate with course, catering, PR, and sponsors

Revenue:
- $1K–$20K+ per event
- Planners often take 10–20% of full budget

10. Golf App or Tech Builder

What You Do:
- Build tools for stat tracking, swing analysis, or scorekeeping
- Or launch a niche app (e.g., Black golfers network, women's tee finder, rangefinder)

Startup Cost:

- Free if DIY, $1K–$5K if hiring a developer

Revenue:

- Subscriptions, licensing, or app store sales
- Scalable to 6–7 figures if built right

The Key: You're Not Competing — You're Creating

There are no gatekeepers in this world.
You don't need a club invite.
You need **a purpose**, **a plan**, and **a platform.**

The fastest-growing lanes in golf are **authentic**, **creative**, and **community-driven.**

Spotlight Story: The Golfer Who Taught The Game Differently

Name: Kendall Green
Hometown: Charlotte, NC
Background: Played D3 golf. Didn't go pro — went grassroots.

Kendall didn't want to just play golf.
She wanted to teach it — but with culture, music, and vibes.

So she created a mobile clinic for girls called **"Tee Like a Queen."**

Her first pop-up had:

- 12 girls
- A DJ
- Water bottles with affirmations
- And custom shirts

She filmed it. Posted it. Tagged local sponsors.

Now?

- She's booked by schools and parks across the South
- Partners with Nike for summer clinics
- Built a brand earning **$8,000+/month**
- Inspiring a generation of young women to walk the fairway with confidence

Real Talk:
"They said golf wasn't for us. So I made it ours."

Playbook Moment:

- Make the game feel like you
- When people feel seen, they show up
- You don't need a scoreboard — you need a service

"You don't need a perfect swing to make an impact. Just a clear purpose and the courage to tee off anyway."

"Golf is slow money — but when it hits, it multiplies with time, trust, and consistency."

Chapter 21

Disrupt The Fairway — How To Make Money From LIV Golf Without Playing

"When golf changed its tone, it opened new doors. The silence is gone — and the money is moving."

The Opportunity: Liv Golf Isn't Just A Tour — It's A Business Model

LIV Golf flipped the script:

- Flashier
- Louder
- Younger
- Global
- Digitally native
- And backed by billions

Whether you agree with how they operate or not, one thing's true: **They created a new economy around golf.**

And like any disruption, it creates **fresh money lanes** for those bold enough to move early.

LIV's Business Ecosystem Is Built For More Than Players

You don't need a swing.
You need:

- A brand
- A service
- A story
- Or a solution

Let's break down the **10 clearest ways to make money in the LIV Golf ecosystem** — from the outside in.

1. Media Creator (Hot Takes, Interviews, Recaps)

What You Do:

- Create content breaking down LIV events, players, behind-the-scenes vibes
- Use YouTube, TikTok, Instagram, or podcasting

Startup Needs:
 Phone, free editing apps, a clear voice

Make Money Through:

- Ads, sponsorships, golf brand deals
- Affiliate links (gear, tech, travel)
- Paid digital products or bonus content

Examples:

- "LIV Tour Weekly" TikTok series
- "Black Golfers React" YouTube channel
- Recaps with edge and culture

2. Travel Experience Consultant / Host

What You Do:

- Plan 3–5 day golf experiences for fans around LIV stops: Flights, hotel, tee times, nightlife, and tournament access

Startup Needs:
Partnerships with hotels, courses, influencers
Booking site or social media presence

How You Get Paid:

- Per head ($500–$2,000/client)
- Referral deals with airlines, brands, local vendors

3. Golf Merch & Apparel Designer (Cultural + Creative)

What You Do:

- Design bold, culture-forward golf streetwear
- Focus on youth, women, minority communities, or LIV-influenced visuals

Startup Needs:
Canva + Print-on-demand store (like Shopify, Teespring)

Revenue Streams:

- Merch drops
- Brand collabs
- Custom orders for leagues or local events

4. Tournament Videographer / Social Clip Editor

What You Do:

- Offer event recap editing for players, influencers, brands, or LIV media teams
- Film cinematic, hype, or lifestyle-style clips

Startup Cost:
$300–$2,000 for a camera kit or mic; or just a phone to start

Pay Range:
$300–$5,000 per project

5. Athlete Brand Strategist / Media Manager

What You Do:

- Manage social, content, and brand deals for LIV players or aspiring pros
- Build their online presence and revenue stream

How to Monetize:

- Retainers ($1K–$3K/month)
- Cut from brand deals (10%–20%)

Who This Works For:

Marketers, creators, or former athletes with branding skill

6. Podcast Host (LIV Culture, Behind-the-Scenes, Fan Talk)

What You Do:

- Launch a show around LIV stories, controversies, lifestyle, fashion, training

Revenue Streams:

- Sponsors (golf, lifestyle, tech)
- Listener support (Patreon, subs)
- Merch or digital products

Topics That Hit:

- LIV vs PGA
- Player interviews
- What golf looks like for new fans

7. Fantasy & Betting Content Creator

What You Do:

- Break down LIV matchups, player stats, odds, and predictions
- Offer paid picks or fantasy strategy

Monetize Through:

- Subscriptions
- Affiliate betting links
- Paid picks/Discord memberships

8. Golf Tech Developer / App Builder

What You Do:

- Create tools for LIV fans or players — stat trackers, swing tools, betting dashboards, social golf apps

Startup Needs:

- Coding skills or developer partners
- $1K–$5K+ startup capital for MVP

Revenue Streams:

- Monthly subscriptions
- App store revenue
- Licensing to golf brands or tournaments

9. Event Vendor / Brand Activation Manager

What You Do:

- Provide food, drinks, merchandise, or services at LIV events
- Create high-engagement brand activations (VIP lounges, giveaways, branded golf carts)

Revenue:
$5K–$50K/event depending on booth, crowd, and partner brands

Who's This For:
Small business owners, marketers, luxury services, mobile entertainment

10. Education & Business of Golf Instructor

What You Do:

- Teach youth, players, or parents the business of golf — NIL, branding, tournament planning, media

Monetize Through:

- Ebooks, courses, webinars, coaching
- Corporate speaking or school programs

Spotlight Story: The Guy Who Flipped the Fairway

Name: Malik Stafford
Hometown: Phoenix, AZ
Background: Grew up playing high school baseball. Switched to golf at 22. Not to play — to tell the story.

Malik saw the rise of LIV and realized there was no one like him reporting on it.
So he launched "Golf Disrupted" — a TikTok/YouTube series focused on:

- Diversity in the game
- LIV player features
- Mic'd up golf culture
- Fit reviews, clubhouse reactions, and hot takes

By year one:

- He gained **80K+ followers**
- Partnered with a mid-level LIV player on content
- Earned **$3K–$8K/month** from brand deals, affiliate links, and merch
- Got flown out to LIV Miami as a guest media voice

Real Talk:
"I didn't need to make the cut. I made content. That's how I got inside."

Playbook Moment:

- Be the voice that's missing
- Find your lane before it's crowded

- When the game evolves, evolve with it

"You don't have to be invited to the tee box to earn off the course. You just have to show up, stay sharp, and build where no one else is swinging."

LIV broke the rules. That means new rules — and new riches — are waiting for you to write them.

Chapter 22

Her Swing, Her Stage — How Women Are Changing The Game And The Business Of Golf

"She doesn't have to swing like them. She just has to show up like herself — and claim the ground that's hers."

The Moment Is Now: Women In Golf Are Rising

For too long, golf told women:

- Don't speak too loud
- Don't wear that
- Don't take up space
- Don't ask for the same checks

That's dead now.

Today, **female golfers and creatives** are:

- Running media platforms
- Launching fashion brands
- Teaching the next generation
- Dominating NIL opportunities
- And flipping the clubhouse into a boardroom

Let's break down **how women — from teens to pros to lifestyle creators — are getting paid off golf** in real ways.

1. College NIL + Social Media Power

Top Players Like:

- Rose Zhang
- Rachel Heck
- Alexa Pano

These women aren't just competing — they're cashing checks:

- **$50K–$300K+ in NIL deals**
- Promoting skincare, golfwear, tech, and sports nutrition
- Using TikTok and Instagram to grow brand value fast

You Don't Need a Full Ride to Eat:

- Mid-level college players are monetizing through:
    - YouTube vlogs
    - Skill reels
    - Lifestyle posts (what's in the bag, practice day routines)
    - Women-in-golf empowerment content

Start With:

- A consistent IG or TikTok theme
- Smart partnerships with women's brands
- Merch, affiliate links, or workshops

2. Hosting Women's Clinics and Confidence Camps

What You Do:

- Create safe, stylish, and welcoming clinics for women of all ages
- Teach golf and mindset: posture, presence, power
- Combine learning with networking, food, fashion, or DJ sets

Why It Works:

- Many women want to learn golf for business, wellness, or social spaces — but they don't want to be judged doing it

Earnings:

- $50–$150 per attendee
- 20–30 women per event
- Multiple clinics = $10K–$30K seasonal income

3. Female-Focused Golf Apparel & Lifestyle Brands

What You Do:

- Design gear for women that fits **our form, style, and movement**
- Create bold slogans, inclusive sizing, and fashion-forward designs

What's Hot:

- Skorts, compression tops, plus-size lines, hijabi-friendly outfits, "golf glam" pieces

Where to Sell:

- Shopify, pop-up events, TikTok Shop, or collabs with golf clubs

Earnings:

- Merch brands can earn $5K–$50K/month if built with the right audience

4. Media Voices, Podcasters, and Creators

Women Are Now:

- Launching golf talk shows
- Reacting to LPGA moments
- Sharing unfiltered practice days

- Covering issues like representation, pay gaps, and mental health

Best Platforms:

- YouTube, Spotify, TikTok
- IG Reels and interviews with other women golfers or business leaders

Revenue Streams:

- Ads, sponsors, NIL brand deals, merch, donations

5. Golf Travel + Experience Hosts for Women

What You Do:

- Plan girls' trips with golf + relaxation + networking
- Mix spa time, scenic courses, brunch, and photo ops

Target Audience:

- Women in business
- Moms rediscovering sports
- Influencers and creators
- Groups looking for golf-with-sisterhood

Pay:

- Trip organizers make $500–$5,000+ per group
- Partner with golf resorts, brands, or tourism boards

6. Golf Coaches and Instructors (Women-Only Focus)

You Can Teach:

- Swing fundamentals
- Golf IQ (rules, etiquette, strategy)
- Business golf prep for executives
- Youth girl players chasing scholarships

Earning Potential:

- $75–$150/hour private sessions

- $2K–$10K per season as a team coach
- Add-ons: online programs, drills, journals, virtual group coaching

7. Building Online Communities + Subscription Clubs

What You Can Do:

- Start a digital sisterhood for women who golf
- Offer:
    - Weekly tips
    - Challenges
    - Live Q&As
    - Gear discounts
    - Group meetups

Tools:

- Patreon, Facebook Groups, Kajabi, or Discord

Revenue:

- $5–$25/month per member
- 100 members = $500–$2,500/month community income

Spotlight Story: The Woman Who Teed Up a Movement

Name: Danielle Thorne
Hometown: Oakland, CA
Background: Played D2 golf. Tired of seeing women fade from the game after college.

Danielle didn't wait for approval.
  She launched **"Play Like Her"** — a mobile golf brand offering:

- Travel clinics for women
- Golf + glam events
- Empowerment interviews with female golfers

- Her own line of functional fashion

She partnered with:

- Callaway (as an ambassador)
- Local Black-owned country clubs
- Women of color in business networks

Now:

- She earns **$15K–$30K/month** through her events, speaking, and merch
- Has a community of 12,000+ women
- Mentors high school girl golfers across the U.S.

Real Talk:

"I got tired of seeing women shrink to fit into golf. So I expanded the space — now we all fit."

Playbook Moment:

- Don't fit in. Build what's missing.
- If the game doesn't feel made for you, make your version of it.

"Her game is bold. Her business is clean. Her swing is soft — but her presence is loud."

The future of golf is female. And profitable. And fearless.

Chapter 23

Bags, Boards & Belief — The Real Power In Golf That Pays For Life

"Some carry clubs. Some close deals. Some walk the fairway with a prayer in their chest. But all of them know: golf opens doors when you learn how to walk through them."

1. The Caddie Economy: From The Bag To The Bank

Before Tiger Woods was a legend, his father taught him what golf could do.
 Before many greats played the Tour, they **carried the clubs** that walked them into it.

Caddying is one of the oldest and most overlooked ways to:

- Get **inside country clubs**
- Learn the **language of golf and wealth**
- And earn **real money** while building reputation

Why Caddying Still Wins:

- **High school/college students** can earn **$100–$500/day**
- At private clubs, caddies get paid **per round + tips + gear perks**

- Caddies often develop **1-on-1 relationships with CEOs, lawyers, investors, and athletes**
- There are even full-ride scholarships (like the **Evans Scholarship**) given to student caddies annually

In a world where most are locked out of elite spaces, the caddie walks right in — and listens.

How to Start as a Caddie:

- Apply at local country clubs or through youth golf nonprofits
- Study yardage books, basic rules, etiquette, and bag setup
- Build a clean appearance, quiet confidence, and excellent listening skills
- Offer to volunteer first, then show value

2. Corporate Golf = Quiet Deals + Big Checks

They say **the real job interview isn't in a boardroom — it's on the back nine.**

Golf is where:

- Partnerships are born
- Sponsorships are negotiated
- Fundraisers turn into investments
- Careers are elevated by proximity

Even if you're not swinging a club, you can still:

- **Host women-in-leadership golf days**
- **Create networking experiences** around scrambles, clinics, or brunch & swing workshops
- **Design merch or manage content** for companies sponsoring charity tournaments
- **Plan team-building retreats** for sales teams or tech startups using golf as the cultural bridge

How Women and Creatives Win in Corporate Golf:

- Start with **community-based clinics** and scale into **professional environments**
- Offer **public speaking, branding,** or **PR services** at golf outings
- Sell your expertise as **"golf culture translation"** — helping companies diversify access

"It's not about golf. It's about what's said during the round — and who feels comfortable being part of it."

3. Faith, Focus & the Inner Game

Golf is more than a sport. It's a **mirror**.

The course reflects your:

- Patience
- Confidence
- Emotional control
- Spiritual trust
- Self-respect under pressure

Many elite golfers lean into:

- **Scripture** (Philippians 4:13 is seen on clubs and gloves)
- **Prayer routines** before key rounds
- **Breathwork or meditation** during mental slumps
- **Journaling wins/losses** with gratitude and lessons

How Faith Shows Up on the Fairway:

- In the silence before a tee shot
- In the decision to try again after a bogey
- In the mindset that **wealth and peace can co-exist**
- In the ability to **compete without ego** and **walk away with grace**

Real Talk:
Golf teaches you that your biggest opponent is never another player — it's the version of yourself that doubts your worth.

Spotlight Story: The Bagman Who Built a Business

Name: Darius Wells
Hometown: Birmingham, AL
Story: Started caddying at 16. Learned the game. Learned the mindset. Listened to every conversation.

Darius kept a notebook in his back pocket.
He wrote down:

- How people talked about money
- What shoes the 6-figure guys wore
- How deals were closed on the 14th green
- What questions made clients open up

At 24, he launched a business planning golf-based experiences for Black executives and young founders.
He now runs:

- **Boardroom on the Tee** — a podcast + digital brand
- **Deals & Divots** — a golf networking summit
- **A leadership program** for high school boys using golf as the anchor

Earnings: $80K/year and growing — but more importantly, **impacting lives and changing access**

Real Talk:
"The first time I carried a bag, I had no clue what was coming. Now I carry the culture forward."

Closing Reflection: Golf's Real Currency Is Access

It's not just a game.
It's a gate.
And once you learn how to swing with **humility, purpose, and**

strategy — you stop asking to enter and start building your own course.

"She stood still. Listened to the wind. Trusted her breath. Swung with love. And broke a legacy wide open."

Golf isn't just where wealth plays. It's where vision walks."

Chapter 24

The Compound Game — Stacking Swings, Stacking Wins

"Golf doesn't reward the fastest. It rewards the most consistent. The quiet work adds up — and one day, it echoes."

Let's Refresh What We Now Know

You've walked through:

The Reality

- Golf is expensive, exclusive, and often misunderstood
- The path to pro is long, political, and unpredictable
- Most won't make the PGA, LPGA, or LIV — but that doesn't mean the game is lost

The Opportunity

- Coaching, camps, clinics, fashion, content, tournaments, apps, NIL, and branding
- Golf is a **global, multi-generational business**
- You can start **young or later in life** and still make a lasting impact

The Power of Presence

- Golf is used in business deals, ministry, mentorship, mental health, therapy, and trust-building
- You can build income and relationships that outlive the scorecard

The Money Moves

- Revenue exists in the shadows: caddying, media, merch, retreats, women's events, partnerships
- If you understand **access > athleticism**, you'll always win

The Compound Effect Of Golf: Why Small Moves Matter

In golf and in life, we're taught to chase the highlight.

But the **real magic lives in the compound moments**:

- That first free clinic you host with 5 girls
- The IG page that only got 23 views in month one
- The YouTube video that barely cracked 100 — but changed someone's life
- The first round of clubs you bought on eBay just to teach your cousin how to hold a grip
- The local park event with borrowed tees and borrowed time

That's where it starts.

And here's what happens:

- One session becomes a movement
- One camp becomes a business
- One podcast becomes a partnership
- One consistent swing becomes legacy

Compound Wins Look Like:

- 100 swings a week = 1K a month = 12K/year
- 10 clinics a year = 200 girls trained = a regional pipeline
- 1 hoodie design every season = 4 drops/year = a brand

- 3 YouTube uploads a month = 36 stories = your proof of concept
- One round with a CEO = one call = one contract = one career

Final Spotlight: The Grandmother Who Changed the Green

Name: Marva Simmons
Hometown: Jackson, MS
Age Started Playing Golf: 52
Background: Church usher. Former high school PE teacher.

Marva joined a ladies' golf group at her church "just to stay active." But she saw how many young Black girls were curious — and how few had access.

So she did something small:
She started **teaching golf every other Saturday at the park.**

No budget.
No brand.
Just a folding table, her old clubs, and a heart big enough to hold 12 girls at a time.

Now?

- She has a nonprofit that's trained over **300+ girls in 3 years**
- Hosts a **"Faith & Fairway" Bible + Golf camp** every summer
- Partners with local schools, sponsors, and small businesses
- **Raised $18K last year alone** to buy gear, snacks, and scholarships
- And gets called "Coach Mama" by girls who never had a safe space before her

Real Talk:
"I didn't know I was building something. I just kept showing up. God did the rest."

Playbook Moment:

- Start late. Start small. Just start.
- Don't build a brand. Build belonging.
- When you love it quietly, it grows loudly.

Closing Reflection: This Is Bigger Than the Swing

This isn't about golf.
This is about what golf teaches us:

- Patience
- Precision
- Presence
- Purpose
- Positioning

It's not about becoming Tiger.

It's about **becoming a light** in a game that wasn't built with us in mind — but will evolve because we stepped in with vision.

"Legacy isn't built in one round — it's stacked through every small swing, every seed you plant, and every person you teach to hold the club with confidence."

Golf is no longer closed. The gate is open. Now walk through it like it's yours."

Chapter 25

Behind The Racket — The Real Game Of Tennis From Youth To Pro

"Tennis is quiet until it isn't. Behind every baseline is a battle — not just for points, but for possibility."

The Myth: Tennis Is A Rich Kid's Sport

There's some truth in it.
The barriers to entry — private lessons, gear, court access, travel tournaments — are high.
 But more and more, **players from humble beginnings** are pushing through and **building legacies**.

Still, to make it?
 You need more than talent. You need strategy, stamina, and sponsorship.

The Numbers: From Youth To Pro

Youth Participation (U.S.)

- Over **4.9 million kids** played tennis in 2023 (USTA)

- Major programs: USTA Junior Circuit, UTR tournaments, National Junior Tennis & Learning (NJTL), private academies

But the dropout rate is high by age 14–16, especially due to:

- High costs
- Lack of scholarships
- Burnout from overtraining
- Lack of local courts in many urban areas

High School Tennis

- ~350,000 total players (boys + girls combined)
- Tennis is available in most public schools — but rarely fully funded
- Many top junior players skip high school teams to focus on **USTA + ITF events** (needed for college and pro ranking points)

College Tennis

- Only **3.3% of high school players** play NCAA
    - 1.1% at D1
    - Others at D2, D3, NAIA, or JUCO
- College tennis can be a **stepping stone to pro** or a gateway to coaching, global travel, and NIL deals

Scholarships (for women) are more plentiful than men

- Men's teams = fewer scholarships, more global competition
- Women's D1 tennis offers **8 full scholarships/team**

Pro Tennis: The Real Funnel

ATP / WTA Tour (Top-Level Pros):

- Top 100 players in the world earn good money
- **Grand Slam winners** earn $2M–$3M per tournament
- Sponsorships can push earnings into **8 figures**

Challenger + ITF Tour (Mid/Entry-Level Pros):

- 90% of players **lose money** at this level
- Prize money is low:
  - $500–$3,000 for many events
  - Travel costs $30K–$80K/year
- Many pros need **family support or private backers** to stay in the game

Turning Pro:

- Some go from **junior ITF** to pro directly
- Others go through **college tennis**, then try Futures and Challenger circuits

Injuries: The Invisible Opponent

Tennis is a **repetitive motion sport**, which means:

- **Chronic overuse injuries** are common
  - Shoulder tendinitis
  - Elbow inflammation (tennis elbow)
  - Knee stress
  - Lower back problems
  - Ankle sprains

Top players travel 10–11 months/year — injuries are as mental as they are physical.

Recovery = lost ranking points + lost income

The Journey In & Out: What It Really Looks Like

In:

- You start at 6–8 years old
- Enter junior tournaments by 9–10
- Train year-round (sometimes homeschool)
- Play national USTA and ITF events
- Spend **$10K–$50K/year** on travel, coaching, gear
- If you're elite, you get college offers or ITF points

- If not, you exit early — or pivot to college club tennis, coaching, or business

Out:

- Many players retire mid-20s if they don't crack the Top 100
- Others transition to:
    - Private coaching ($75–$150/hr)
    - College coaching (D1 assistants earn $60K–$150K+)
    - Tennis academy founders
    - Fitness training
    - Equipment brands
    - Content creation
    - Tournament direction

Global Nature Of The Sport = Global Opportunities

- 70% of D1 tennis players are international
- Tennis is popular in **Europe, Asia, South America, and Africa**
- You can build a business or brand in **travel, bilingual training, or international recruiting**

Where The Wins Are (Even Without Going Pro):

- Tennis camps + clinics for kids in underserved areas
- Branded online content (YouTube breakdowns, strategy guides, fitness programs)
- Organizing recreational leagues for adults or schools
- NIL and personal branding for college players
- College tennis consulting (recruiting help for parents)
- Tennis therapy & mental wellness programs
- Crossover programs (tennis + music, yoga, business)

"The court is small, but the world around it is massive — and it pays those who know how to play the long game."

Chapter 26

The Other Court — How To Make Money In Tennis Without Going Pro

"You don't need a trophy to win. You just need a plan, a purpose, and the courage to build around the game you love."

The Truth:

Only a tiny percentage of tennis players will ever see Centre Court at Wimbledon.

But here's the twist:

The business of tennis is way bigger than the rankings.

You don't have to be Serena, Federer, or Djokovic to make six figures.
You need a clear lane, consistent moves, and a plan that plays to your strengths.

Let's break down **10 proven ways to make money in tennis —** no pro card required.

1. Private Coaching or Group Training

What You Do:

- Teach kids, teens, or adults basic skills, footwork, mental focus, or elite strategy

Startup Tools:

- Courts at parks or schools
- Your racquet, cones, and knowledge

Rates:

- $50–$150/hour private lessons
- $25–$75 per person for small groups

Scale It:

- Offer monthly memberships
- Create weekend clinics
- Host online virtual sessions

2. Start a Tennis Academy or Camp Series

What You Do:

- Build a seasonal or year-round program focused on development, fun, or competition

Best For:

- Former college players, experienced coaches, or passionate leaders

Revenue:

- 20 players × $250/month = $5K/month
- Summer camps = $5K–$20K per session

Bonus:

- Partner with schools, parks, nonprofits

3. Tennis Content Creator (YouTube, TikTok, IG)

What You Do:

- Share drills, breakdowns, match reactions, equipment reviews, mic'd up sessions, and culture

Startup Tools:

- Smartphone + editing app (CapCut, InShot, iMovie)

Monetization:

- YouTube ads, IG bonuses, brand sponsorships, affiliate links, digital products

Niche Ideas:

- "Tennis for Beginners"
- "Street Court Tennis Stories"
- "College Match Commentary"
- "Black Girl Serve Game"
- "Tennis + Fashion Series"

4. Tennis Event Organizer / League Director

What You Do:

- Create local leagues, weekend round robins, charity tournaments, or adult play nights

Startup Cost:

- $250–$1,000 (permits, flyers, snacks, prizes)

Revenue:

- 50 players × $25–$50 entry = $1K–$2.5K/weekend
- Add food vendors, photographers, merch, DJs

Scale It:

- Build a citywide or school-based circuit
- Offer an "elite vs amateur" series

5. Tennis Apparel, Merch, and Gear Brand

What You Do:

- Design clothing, headbands, grip wraps, or court bags for players with style

Theme Ideas:
- "Racquet Royalty"
- "Serve First. Talk Later."
- "Court Queens"
- "Baseline Hustle"
- "Clay Over Chaos"

Use Platforms:
- Shopify, Printful, Teespring

Revenue:
- Merch brands = $500–$20K/month with the right niche + promo

6. NIL Consulting or Personal Branding for Tennis Players

What You Do:
- Help junior or college players grow their IG, negotiate deals, launch merch, or create content

Best For:
- Creatives, marketers, or former athletes

How to Monetize:
- $100–$300/hour
- Retainer clients
- Digital product sales

7. Tennis Performance Coach (Fitness + Mental Game)

What You Do:

- Train players on speed, footwork, nutrition, mindset, and recovery
- Offer strength plans, mental reps, or pre-match routines

Certs Help:

- NASM, TPI, or sports psych background

Make Money Through:

- 1-on-1 coaching
- Team consulting
- Online programs

8. Tennis Podcast or Blog

What You Cover:

- Match analysis, interviews, tennis culture, global stories, wellness, gear

Tools Needed:

- Anchor, Spotify, or YouTube
- Canva or Substack for newsletters

Monetization:

- Sponsors, affiliate links, subscriber bonuses

Ideas:

- "The Tennis Table Talk"
- "Voices from the Baseline"
- "Inside the ITF Grind"
- "Black Tennis Journal"

9. Tennis Photographer or Videographer

What You Do:

- Shoot tournaments, profile players, create social content, document training

Pay Rates:

- $200–$1,000 per shoot
- Highlight reels for recruiting = $150–$500

You Can Work With:

- Schools
- Clubs
- Influencers
- Parents

10. College Tennis Recruiting Consultant

What You Do:

- Guide players + families through scholarship process, video creation, timelines, and school matching

Great For:

- Former players or coaches

Rates:

- $500–$2,000 packages
- Create a course + sell at scale

Spotlight Story: The Coach Who Served Purpose

Name: Marisol Reyes
Hometown: El Paso, TX
Background: Former D2 college player. Never went pro. But she built something bigger.

After coaching part-time, Marisol saw how few Latinas were represented in competitive tennis.
 So she started **"La Fuerza Tennis"** — a brand and camp series focused on empowering young girls through tennis + identity.

Now?

- Hosts 3 clinics a year in Texas and Arizona
- Sells merch that says "Power. Precision. Pride."
- Speaks at college athlete summits
- Makes **$6,000–$12,000 per event season**
- Coaches privately on the side
- Building a YouTube channel to highlight Latina players

Real Talk:
"I don't need to be on the tour. I am the tour in my community."

Playbook Moment:
- Tennis was her tool.
- Legacy was her goal.
- She serves differently — and it's changing lives.

"You don't need ranking points to be impactful. You just need a lane, a rhythm, and the will to keep serving purpose, one swing at a time."

Chapter 27

Serve & Earn — The Real Revenue In Tennis And How To Tap In

"You don't need a trophy to win. You just need a plan, a purpose, and the courage to build around the game you love."

Tennis is a multi-billion-dollar global industry. Every year, the sport generates more than nine billion dollars across player earnings, events, sponsorships, travel, gear, coaching, fashion, and content. The headlines go to the Grand Slam champions and ATP/WTA elites—but beneath that spotlight is a quiet world of people making **real money** off tennis without ever going pro.

If you love the game, you can get paid. And not just a little.

Whether you're a solid recreational player, a former high school athlete, a parent, a creative, or a part-time coach, you can build a lane that pays you back consistently. But you have to stop thinking like a fan—and start thinking like a builder.

Let's talk revenue, reality, and routes.

The most direct and scalable lane is coaching. A private tennis coach can earn anywhere from $50 to $150 per hour depending on location and experience. If you do just ten hours a week at $75, you're looking at nearly $40,000 per year part-time. Double that? You're over $70K without working full-time hours. Group training can take it further. Coaching four players at $40 each gives you $160 an hour. Build a reputation at the park, local schools, or community centers, and you've got a long-term revenue stream built on skill, service, and trust.

Then you have tennis camps and clinics. Hosting a youth camp for $200 per person with just 20 kids brings in $4,000 per session. Run four sessions across summer and fall and you're adding another $15,000 or more. Adults also pay for structured weekend skill camps, cardio tennis, and doubles strategy sessions. These camps can be casual or advanced—what matters is consistency, branding, and experience.

If you're more content-driven, tennis is wide open. Create a YouTube or TikTok channel reviewing racquets, showing technique drills, breaking down matches, or simply documenting your journey. It doesn't take millions of views to monetize. With YouTube ads, affiliate links to tennis gear, brand sponsorships, and eBooks, even a modest following can bring in thousands. Tennis fans want personality and insight, not perfection. Start where you are.

You can also go the fashion route. Players love gear that reflects their vibe—especially the new generation. Launching a small apparel brand with slogans like "Baseline Hustle," "Serve Strong," or "Court Queen" can create identity and income. Using print-on-demand sites like Printful and Shopify, you don't even need upfront inventory. A few clean designs and some creative promotion could land you in the $5K to $20K range annually—or more if you hit the right market.

Tennis events offer another revenue play. Hosting your own tournament, round-robin league, or weekend doubles event brings in real returns. Charge players $30 to $50 to enter. With 40 participants, that's $1,200 to $2,000 in a single weekend. Add food vendors, custom shirts, medals, and you've just created a business model that feeds the local tennis community—and your bank account.

If you're into photography or video, there's a lane for you too. Tennis parents pay good money for highlight videos, college recruiting footage, and tournament photos. Shooting 3–5 matches a weekend, charging $250 per package, adds up quickly. Videographers and editors who focus on tennis can easily earn $10K to $50K per year on the side—or more with consistent marketing.

For those who love organization and access, recruiting consultation is a real opportunity. Help young players and their families understand how to get noticed by college coaches. Provide services like email scripting, timeline planning, video editing, and even NIL branding. You don't need a huge client list to win—ten clients paying $1,000 each is a $10,000 lane that helps kids and pays your purpose forward.

Now picture this:

You coach ten hours a week. You run two weekend clinics every quarter. You launch a merch line with three shirt designs. You post weekly videos about your journey. You host one local tournament in spring and another in fall. Stack that across twelve months and you're realistically pulling in $50,000 to $75,000—without ever swinging a racquet at Wimbledon.

And that's just a starting point.

Spotlight Story: Keith Nolan – The Weekend Player Who Made It Pay

Keith Nolan grew up playing tennis in Cleveland. He never played college ball. He didn't get a scholarship. No national ranking. But he loved the game. After high school, he got a job in IT. On Saturdays, he'd head to the public park, hit with friends, sometimes play pickup doubles with whoever showed up. One afternoon, a father asked him to help his son with serve form. Keith said yes. That yes became a second student. Then five. Then ten.

He got certified, built a website, started a weekend training group called **Serve Strong Saturdays**. He ran clinics every quarter, launched a clean merch line with simple black-and-white hoodies, and began posting tips and drills on YouTube. In one year, he generated more than $47,000 through coaching, camps, content, and shirts. All while working his day job.

Keith didn't need to make it to the pros. He made it right where he was. And his love for the game became a financial foundation.

"I used to just hit on Saturdays. Now I coach, create, and sell gear—and I love it more than ever."

You don't have to play on center court to win. You just have to learn how the court works, how the business moves, and where you fit inside it. Every serve, every drill, every bit of value you offer has a ripple effect. You can build your own system. You can serve in your own way.

If you move with intention and strategy, tennis can give you joy, freedom, income, and influence.

"The court is only one part of the game. When you learn the business around the net—you serve your way into profit, purpose, and peace."

Chapter 28

The Pickleball Wave — History, Hustle, and the New Money Game

"It started as a backyard game. Now it's a billion-dollar wave. The question isn't 'can I go pro?' It's 'how can I build with it?'"

The game was born in 1965, on Bainbridge Island, Washington, when three dads improvised a game to entertain their kids. They used ping pong paddles, a wiffle ball, and a lowered badminton net. What started as family fun eventually took shape as **pickleball**—a quirky mix of tennis, ping pong, and badminton that's **now one of the most played and profitable sports in the country**.

For decades, pickleball grew slowly through retirement communities and local parks. But in the last five years, everything changed. Post-pandemic recreation boomed. Influencers started filming matches. Celebrities like LeBron James, Tom Brady, and Drake bought into professional pickleball teams. Brands flooded in. Now, the sport has transformed into a cultural and commercial movement.

The Numbers: Pickleball's Growth Is Unmatched

There are now **more than 36.5 million players in the U.S. alone**. That's more than baseball. More than golf. More than any other paddle sport. And it's **growing at over 150% per year**, with no signs of slowing down.

In 2023 alone:

- Pickleball prize money passed $10 million.
- Private clubs, tournaments, and leagues popped up in every major city.
- Real estate investors started converting abandoned retail spaces into indoor pickleball venues.
- The sport's global reach began expanding into Canada, Asia, and the Caribbean.

Where The Money Is

You don't have to be a pro to get paid.

Here's how **everyday players, coaches, entrepreneurs, and creatives** are making money right now from the pickleball boom:

First, **coaching**. Many former tennis and racquetball players are shifting into pickleball instruction. You don't need pro-level skills—just certification, communication, and consistency. Private pickleball coaches earn $50 to $125 per hour, and group sessions (4–8 players) pay even more per hour when stacked right. Some instructors are pulling in $60K to $100K a year, running clinics at local parks and clubs.

Then there's the rise of **pickleball tournaments and leagues**. Recreational players are showing up in huge numbers to compete at amateur events—many paying $25 to $75 in entry fees. Hosting a round-robin tournament with 100 players can generate $5,000 or more in a weekend, especially when paired with sponsors, food vendors, or merchandise.

Next is **content creation**. Social media is filled with highlight reels, funny moments, mic'd up doubles matches, and beginner tips. If you start a channel offering consistent, niche content—whether you're a ref, coach, or just a hype voice—you can monetize through ads, brand partnerships, and affiliate gear links. Some creators are already making $2K to $10K a month by simply documenting what's happening in local games and tournaments.

You can also build a **pickleball apparel or gear brand**. Think paddle bags, gloves, visors, streetwear-style shirts, or slogans like "Dink God," "Kitchen Control," or "No Bounce Back." Use print-on-demand platforms and target local clubs or Facebook groups to scale slowly. Fashion and function both matter here, especially to younger, style-conscious players.

There's also big opportunity in **pickleball club management** and facility ownership. Entrepreneurs are converting empty warehouses or malls into high-end pickleball clubs with food, drinks, and social energy. These locations often charge $10–$20 per player per hour, host weekly events, and sell memberships. While real estate investment takes capital, even being the event planner, club manager, or league organizer at one of these spaces can be a six-figure role.

And don't forget **training tools, digital apps, and tournament software**. With more games being played, tools that help track stats, organize brackets, livestream matches, or coach virtually are becoming valuable. Developers and digital creators can build for this growing community and monetize through subscriptions or partnerships.

What Makes Pickleball Different

This sport doesn't require elite genetics, million-dollar training, or Olympic-level conditioning. It welcomes all ages, body types, and skill levels. That's why it grows fast—and why it's open to innovation.

It's casual enough for your aunt to play, but competitive enough for college athletes to dominate. It lives in parks, but it's moving into luxury spaces. That blend of **accessibility and culture** is why money is flowing in every direction.

If you can:

- Teach,
- Plan,
- Create,
- Record,
- Design,
- Organize,
- Or brand something...

You can eat off this wave.

Spotlight Story: Simone Hall – From Stay-At-Home Mom To Pickleball Powerhouse

Simone was a former high school tennis player from Charlotte. She left the game behind after college, had three kids, and was working part-time in accounting. Then one afternoon, her neighbor invited her to play a game called pickleball.

She got hooked immediately.

Within six months, Simone got certified and started teaching a weekly beginner clinic at her local YMCA. Then she created an Instagram page called **"PickleMama"**—sharing tips, funny court moments, and reels of her journey. She began selling t-shirts with slogans like "Kitchen Queen" and "No Dink Left Behind."

Today, Simone:

- Teaches three group classes a week.
- Hosts monthly women-only doubles events.
- Runs an email list of 2,500 players in her region.
- Makes over $60,000 a year from coaching, merch, and content—while still making time for her family.

"I didn't see myself in the sport. So I made space. And now I run that space with love."

Her paddle didn't take her to the pros. It took her to freedom.

Pickleball is still young. That means there's no blueprint—just blank space. That's your opportunity. You don't need to be a legend to win. You just need to show up early, move with intention, and find your serve.

Because this isn't just a sport. It's a moment. And you can build with it.

"This time, the net isn't a barrier. It's a bridge. Pick up your paddle, bring your idea, and meet the moment."

Tierre Ford

Chapter 29

The Global Game — Inside the Numbers of Soccer's Reach and Rise

"You don't need to wear the jersey to win in this game. You just need to understand the pitch—and know where to move when no one's watching."

Let's be clear: **soccer is the most played sport on Earth**.

Over 250 million people actively play soccer worldwide, with **over 4 billion fans**—making it the largest single-sport audience on the planet. From dusty backstreets in Lagos to the stadiums of Spain, from U.S. high school fields to Brazilian favelas—soccer isn't just a sport, it's a **language**, a **lifestyle**, and for many, a **way out**.

In the United States, the soccer wave is surging. Youth participation is higher than baseball. The MLS is expanding. Women's soccer is one of the strongest, most decorated programs in the country. And international clubs are planting roots in American soil to tap into talent and fan money.

But with all that growth comes a reality check: **only a small fraction make it to the top**.

Youth To Pro: The Soccer Funnel

In the U.S. alone, over **3 million kids** are registered in organized youth soccer each year. Thousands more play casually, in afterschool programs, city leagues, or just wherever a ball can bounce.

By high school, roughly **850,000 players** suit up across boys' and girls' teams. That sounds big—until you zoom in.

Only about **5% of high school soccer players** go on to play in college. Even fewer—less than 1%—will get drafted to MLS, NWSL, or play professionally overseas. And for those who do, only the elite of the elite make life-changing money. The rest are grinding it out in lower divisions, semi-pro leagues, or chasing contracts season to season.

Globally, the numbers are even sharper. **Most top-tier footballers are scouted between ages 12 and 16**. Academies across Europe, South America, and Africa develop young players with military-level precision—but the cutthroat nature means one injury, one bad season, or one missed opportunity can derail the dream.

The Global Money: What's Really Moving

Soccer's revenue is staggering. FIFA generated over **$7.6 billion in 2022**, mostly from World Cup licensing, broadcasting, and sponsorships. Top clubs like Real Madrid, Manchester United, and PSG operate as billion-dollar global brands. Player transfers exceed **$10 billion annually**, with deals like Neymar's $263M transfer reshaping markets.

The Premier League alone brings in **over $6 billion a year**, while players like Lionel Messi, Cristiano Ronaldo, and Kylian Mbappé earn **$50M–$150M+ annually** between contracts and endorsements.

But the money doesn't stop at the top. It filters down through:

- Local club team academies
- Travel soccer organizations
- Coaches and trainers
- Apparel companies
- Sports data and analytics
- Agents and scouting services
- Streaming platforms and content creators
- Social media commentary, grassroots brands, and tournament hosts

There are **thousands of ways the soccer economy pays**—but very few people outside the spotlight ever talk about them.

The U.S. Soccer Landscape

Major League Soccer (MLS) now has **29 teams** and is expanding. The league is investing in player development, media rights, and stadium experiences. In 2023, Apple signed a **$2.5 billion streaming deal** with MLS, showing how digital access is rewriting the game.

The **NWSL** (National Women's Soccer League) is also gaining traction, with stronger attendance, new investors, and major brand sponsorships. U.S. Women's National Team legends like Alex Morgan and Megan Rapinoe helped shift public opinion, and now younger stars are bringing style, social media presence, and global influence.

Youth academies tied to pro teams are becoming more common, but access is still unequal. Many families can't afford the pay-to-play model of elite club soccer, which often runs $2,000–$5,000+ per year just for tournament travel and training. That means **too many gifted players never get seen—not because of talent, but because of economics**.

The Injuries And Grind

Soccer may look smooth on the surface, but the grind is real. Common injuries include torn ACLs, ankle sprains, hamstring pulls, and overuse issues like shin splints or lower back pain. Add in the emotional pressure, the constant competition, and the early burnout—and many talented players walk away by age 18.

Globally, soccer academies run like businesses. They develop hundreds of kids for every one who gets a professional contract. Most of those who don't make it are left with no plan, no income, and sometimes, no identity.

The Reality Check

Even if you make it to the pros, contracts can be short, team loyalty thin, and backup players often earn far less than the stars. Most MLS players earn between **$80K and $150K/year**—solid, but not generational wealth. Lower-division or overseas contracts can be much smaller.

That's why **understanding the full system—not just the game—is key.**

Because for every Messi, there are 1,000 coaches, trainers, tournament organizers, analysts, content creators, and gear makers eating off the same sport. The spotlight is narrow—but the business is wide open.

"Soccer is global. The ball doesn't need batteries. The game needs no translation. It connects people faster than language and spreads faster than news."

Chapter 30

The Other Goal — How To Make Money From Soccer Without Going Pro

"You don't need a contract to get paid. You just need a vision, consistency, and the courage to build around the game you love."

Soccer isn't just a sport. It's an economy.

It's woven into culture, fashion, travel, education, digital media, and identity.

Even if you never play for a team, you can still build a future in the game. From running youth programs to producing soccer content to designing merch, the opportunities are endless when you learn where the money flows.

Let's walk through the **real ways regular people are getting paid in soccer**—and how you can too.

Private Coaching And Small Group Training

One of the most accessible ways to earn is through private and group sessions. If you know the game, you can coach it. Parents pay anywhere from $30 to $100+ per hour for 1-on-1 sessions, especially in competitive areas. Group sessions are even more profitable—six players at $25 each is $150 an hour.

You don't need to be a pro. You just need communication skills, drills, structure, and patience. Offer development for kids, positional clinics (like striker or defender work), fitness-focused training, or speed/agility programs. You can run sessions at local parks, school fields, or rent turf during off-hours.

Launch A Youth Soccer Camp Or Clinic Series

If you've got experience, even at the high school or college level, you can host local camps. A two-day clinic charging $100 per player with 30 players is $3,000 in one weekend. Add guest coaches, branded t-shirts, or parent Q&As and you've created something valuable and scalable.

Do it once per quarter and you're now making an extra $12K–$15K a year—on your own schedule.

Create Soccer Content

Soccer is global. That means the **audience is massive**.

Start a YouTube or TikTok channel breaking down goals, reacting to matches, telling street soccer stories, or interviewing youth players and coaches. There are channels built around cleat reviews, FIFA pack openings, "how to curve the ball," or "5 drills to train at home." Monetize through ads, merch, or affiliate links to gear.

Even a small audience can earn. Some creators make $500 to $5,000+ per month just talking about the sport they love.

Merch And Streetwear Inspired By Soccer Culture

From jerseys to slogans to custom scarves and lifestyle shirts, soccer fashion is booming. Whether you're targeting local fans or building a global niche brand, design gear that speaks to culture, pride, or community.

You can drop small batches with slogans like:

- "Ball Is My Passport"
- "Respect the Pitch"
- "Shooters Gonna Shoot"
- "Midfield Minds Club"

Use print-on-demand platforms to start with little cost and promote through your IG or YouTube.

Tournament Organizer Or League Director

Soccer tournaments are big business—even at the amateur level. Host your own small-sided league, weekend futsal tournaments, or youth competitions. Charge registration fees, partner with local vendors, sell branded shirts, and get sponsors.

One local tournament with 20 teams at $200 per team = $4,000. Do it quarterly, and you've built a $16K+ side business.

Become A Soccer Photographer Or Videographer

Offer highlight reels for high school and college players. Parents will pay for recruiting videos, and clubs will hire creators to film events. A single highlight reel package can go for $200–$500.

Shoot training sessions, create mini-docs, or run a sports storytelling page and earn through content sales or sponsorships.

Build A Soccer Skills App Or Online Program

If you have drills, strategy, and teaching ability, package it. Create an online course, sell a $29 ball-control eBook, or build an app that helps kids train at home. Parents love tools that keep their kids engaged and improving.

You can film everything from your phone and use platforms like Gumroad, Teachable, or even WhatsApp to deliver lessons.

Offer College Recruitment Or NIL Guidance

Many players and families don't understand how college soccer recruiting works. If you've been through the process, you can teach it. Offer Zoom consultations, edit email templates, help players build highlight reels, or guide them through the scholarship process.

Charge $100–$500 per package or run small workshops in your area.

Referee Certification And League Work

Becoming a certified soccer ref can earn you $30–$100 per game depending on age and level. Ref 5–10 games on a weekend and you've added hundreds per week to your income—plus, it's a great way to stay connected to the game.

International Travel And Tour Hosting

Plan soccer travel trips abroad. Offer cultural tours to Spain, Brazil, or Ghana. Partner with academies to give players overseas exposure. You can make money by coordinating the experience, booking travel, or serving as a translator or organizer.

Spotlight Story: Coach D – The King Of Local Pitch Hustle

Derrick "Coach D" Maxwell never went pro. He played JUCO, did two years at a D2 school, then walked away from competitive play. But he didn't walk away from the game.

In his city, he started coaching for a club team. But he noticed a gap—tons of kids loved the game but couldn't afford club fees. So he started his own program. He trained kids in the park. He filmed workouts and posted them on IG. He hosted free clinics, then small events. Word spread.

Now? Coach D trains over 50 kids per week. He runs a quarterly camp that brings in $6,000 per session. He's dropped a cleat bag line. He makes $2,000 a month from content and consults with four different local clubs. Total: over $75,000 a year. All from a game he didn't "make it" in.

"I didn't need a contract. I built my own system. I don't chase teams. I lead one."

The ball might be round, but your path doesn't have to be. If you love the game, you can serve, build, teach, host, coach, or create your way into a lane that pays. The dream isn't gone—it just looks different.

"Soccer doesn't just belong to pros. It belongs to those who make the culture, build the pitch, and keep the game alive. Play smart—and build where you stand."

Chapter 31

Beyond the Pitch — Closing the Soccer Section with Power, Vision, and Legacy

"Some score goals. Others build the field. Either way, they change the game."

Soccer doesn't just belong to the pros.

It belongs to the uncle coaching five kids at the park with cones made from old water bottles.
 To the sister filming highlight reels on her iPhone to get her brother recruited.
 To the trainer running speed drills before work, making sure every kid with no ride still gets better.
 To the high school grad printing T-shirts with hometown slogans, flipping culture into currency.

This game belongs to those who **refused to let a closed door define their finish line**.

That's what this section has been about.

The Recap: All the Ways the Game Pays

You've seen the blueprint. Let's remind them how deep the system goes:

There's money in:

- Private sessions—working with five players a week at $50/hour
- Youth clinics—charging $100 per player with 20 kids each weekend
- Travel team consulting—helping parents navigate club politics and scholarships
- Tournament hosting—20 local teams paying $200 each to compete
- Branded gear—merchandise that speaks to your region, your roots, your rhythm
- Soccer content—breakdowns, interviews, stories, skills, and player reactions
- NIL and recruiting help—guiding youth athletes through social branding and scholarship steps
- Photography and editing—capturing and crafting college-ready highlight reels
- Referee work—certified and paid for youth, high school, and adult leagues
- Global pathways—organizing international player tours or exchange clinics
- Even running a soccer podcast or local media page—monetizing attention and access

Each of those can stand alone. Or stack.

The Math: Compound Movement

Let's say you run ten sessions a week at $50/hour. That's $500/week.

Now add two weekend clinics per month at $2,000 each =

$4,000/month
 Drop a shirt line that nets $1,000/month
 Add content income of $500/month
 Ref four games a week at $60/game = $960/month

That's over $80,000 a year. From serving, not shining.

That's the other goal.

The Mission: What It Really Means

This isn't just about money.

It's about **ownership**.

Too often, Black and Brown players are the faces of talent, but not the owners of teams.
 We're seen on the field, but not behind the clinics. In the jerseys, but not in the contracts.

That's changing.

When you build programs, train others, create brands, and monetize your culture—you rewrite what power looks like in this game.

You create a new generation that doesn't just want to play... but wants to **own**, **lead**, and **build**.

Spotlight Story: Edwin Martinez — The Man Who Built A Lane

Edwin never went D1. He played pick-up in the Bronx, coached rec league, and worked nights at a UPS warehouse. But he noticed something—there were no affordable programs for immigrant kids. No one teaching them how to train, how to get seen, or how to take soccer seriously.

So he started a 5-person clinic in a church parking lot.

Two years later, he launched **"Goal Within Reach,"** a nonprofit that trains over 1,200 youth per year in four boroughs.

He partnered with Nike. He pays teens to coach so they don't have to hustle. He runs mental health check-ins, SAT prep, and financial literacy courses—through soccer.

Last year, he cleared $180,000 in donations, grants, brand partnerships, and merchandise.

Edwin didn't get a contract. He **built his contract**.

"I was never gonna make the national team. So I built something that makes sure the next generation could."

The pitch is only one part of the game.
The real power lives in the people who keep it alive after the lights go out.

You don't need to be the star.
You just need to **serve, see what's missing**, and **stand where legacy can grow.**

You can make money, make purpose, and make room—for yourself and for others.

Because soccer is still being written.
The ball is still moving.
And the field is still wide open.

"You don't have to play for the jersey to make history. You just have to make space, make an impact, and make sure your people are never left out of the game again."

Chapter 32

Lanes Of Truth — The Track From Youth To Pro

"Some run for time. Some run for life. But the real win is learning how to make your pace pay—long after the clock stops."

Track and field is the original proving ground.

Before contracts, before hype, before lights—there was a line, a lane, and a finish.

It's one of the most powerful tools in underserved communities. It requires no fancy equipment. No expensive team fees. No politics—just **work**, **discipline**, and **execution**.

But here's what they don't always tell you:
 Less than 1% of all track athletes make a living running full-time.

The spotlight is real. But the system is quiet. And if you don't understand both, you can chase greatness and still come up short—financially, mentally, and emotionally.

Youth Participation

In the U.S., over **1 million kids** participate in youth track and field annually through AAU, USATF, and middle school leagues. It's one of the fastest-growing entry-level sports due to low costs and accessibility.

By high school, nearly **1 million students** run track—more than football and basketball combined. Track is especially strong among Black youth, particularly in urban areas, where it often serves as a gateway to college exposure and structure.

But by college, the numbers shrink fast.

College-Level Competition

Only around **6% of high school track athletes** go on to compete in college.

- Division I programs are highly competitive.
- Scholarships are often partial—not full rides.
- Roster spots are limited and mostly go to sprinters, hurdlers, jumpers, and distance specialists with elite state/national-level times.

Most college track athletes juggle academics, training, and limited travel stipends—many without NIL deals or long-term support.

And then... there's the pro level.

The Harsh Reality Of Pro Track

Track is an Olympic sport—but outside of Olympic years, there's limited visibility.

Only **the top 0.5% of runners in the world** are making six-figure contracts from brands like Nike, Adidas, Puma, or New Balance.

Let's break it down:

- A few dozen elite sprinters, hurdlers, and distance runners earn $100K–$500K/year (including bonuses and endorsements).
- Medal winners at major championships (Olympics, World Champs) earn prize money and sponsorship bonuses.
- Many other pro runners earn **less than $30K/year**, living off appearance fees, minor sponsorships, and hustling camps or merch to make it work.

Women and field athletes—especially throwers—are often paid even less.

To stay "pro," most athletes train 30+ hours/week, work side jobs, and travel on their own dime just to chase qualifying times.

Injuries And Burnout

Track is brutal on the body.

Common injuries include hamstring tears, shin splints, tendonitis, stress fractures, hip flexor issues, and spinal compression—especially among sprinters, hurdlers, and jumpers. Rehab can derail an entire season. One injury can cost a contract or Olympic dream.

Burnout is just as real.

Many elite runners hit their physical peak before 25. And without support systems—mentally, financially, or emotionally—many fade out early, even after national-level success.

The International Scene

Globally, the U.S., Jamaica, Kenya, Ethiopia, and the U.K. dominate elite-level track. But opportunities vary by region.

- In the Caribbean and parts of Africa, top runners may be national heroes—but lack consistent funding or exposure.
- In Europe and Asia, track is respected—but often overshadowed by soccer or basketball.

- U.S.-based college scholarships remain a top target for global talent.

More than ever, international athletes are using track as a **bridge**—not just to competition, but to education, branding, and travel.

The Money Breakdown

The average **non-sponsored pro athlete** earns $0–$25K/year.

Top **Olympians** can clear **$250K–$1M+ in a peak year**, depending on medals, appearances, and deals.

Shoe contracts vary wildly—some as low as $5K/year, others with heavy performance bonuses.

Prize money for Diamond League meets is solid ($10K+ for 1st place), but the competition is elite-only.

In other words: **there's money—but it's scarce, streaky, and mostly concentrated at the very top.**

Final Truth: The Clock Isn't Your Only Metric

The biggest myth in track is that **speed is the only way to win.**

But speed fades. Fame fades. Contracts expire.

The athletes who thrive long-term are the ones who learn to:

- Teach the game
- Brand themselves
- Host clinics and camps
- Create digital training content
- Speak, coach, or build platforms that go beyond their time

Spotlight Story: Rayna Jefferson – From State Champion To Community Champion

Rayna Jefferson was a four-time state champion sprinter out of Baton Rouge, Louisiana. She ran a 11.55 in the 100m as a senior, earning her a partial scholarship to a D1 school. Everyone thought she was next up.

But sophomore year, her hamstring tore—badly. She tried to rehab, came back too soon, and tore it again.

By junior year, her scholarship was cut, and her dreams of going pro disappeared.

But Rayna didn't disappear.

Instead of chasing a comeback, she pivoted.

She started mentoring younger girls on campus. She became a student assistant for the team, learned how to coach sprints, and after graduation, she launched her own speed academy—**Jet Lane Training**.

She bought cones, ladders, and two portable speakers. She trained kids at public parks on weekends, recording drills on Instagram, and breaking down mechanics in simple language that parents could understand.

Two years later, Rayna:

- Trains 40 athletes per week
- Runs a summer sprint camp for 100+ youth
- Created an online course on sprint form and injury prevention
- Sells hoodies with her slogan: "Run It With Purpose"
- Makes over **$85K/year** doing what she loves—without ever going pro

"My injury took me off the track. But it didn't take the track out of me. I just changed lanes."

Some athletes chase medals. Others chase meaning. Rayna found both—by shifting her stride from personal glory to generational impact.

Tierre Ford

"When the stopwatch stopped, her purpose started."

You don't have to chase the stopwatch forever.
You can run your own race.

Chapter 33

From the Sideline — Where the Real Track Money Lives

"You may not be on the line when the gun goes off, but you can still control the race if you know how to move behind the scenes."

Track is a sport where 90% of the attention goes to the top 1% of athletes.

But here's what most people miss:

The real money is in the sideline—coaching, creating, organizing, building.

From youth meets to Olympic trials, there are people all around the edges of the sport making steady, powerful income.

Let's break the numbers down.

Private Coaching And Speed Training

Speed is a skill every athlete wants—football players, soccer players, hoopers, and even wrestlers. That makes sprinters and hurdlers some of the most in-demand trainers in sports.

Many private track coaches charge $50 to $150 per hour for sessions.
Run 10 sessions a week at $75/hr and you're making $3,000/month—over $36K a year, part-time.
Group training boosts it further. Four athletes at $40 each = $160/hr.
Train teams, youth programs, or pair it with strength and conditioning for even more value.

Track Camps, Clinics, and Workshops

Host a weekend clinic at a school or park. Charge $100 per athlete.
Get 30 athletes = $3,000 in one weekend.
Do that quarterly? You're making $12K–$15K per year just on in-person training events.

Specialty workshops work too:

- Start Block Masterclass
- Hurdle Technique & Form
- Long Jump Mechanics
- How to Cut Time in 4 Weeks

Build a brand around your zone of expertise and scale it city to city or online.

Online Programs and Digital Products

Package what you know into an online course, downloadable eBook, or video tutorial series. You can sell:

- Sprint mechanics guides
- Speed training workouts
- Form correction series
- Nutrition and race prep checklists
- "How to Earn a Track Scholarship" guides for parents

Price it between $29–$99 and start selling to your IG audience, YouTube subscribers, or through email marketing.

Sell 300 eBooks at $40 and you've made $12,000 without leaving your house.

Merch And Apparel Built For The Culture

Track athletes are underrepresented in lifestyle merch—but they have strong pride and identity. Create gear with messages like:

- "Keep Your Form. Kill Your Lane."
- "I Run My Race."
- "Sprinter State of Mind"
- "Last Heat, Best Heat"
- "Field Event Royalty"

Even a small merch brand can generate $500–$5,000/month if marketed well—especially if tied to your clinic, content, or local reputation.

Content Creation: Coaching, Motivation, And Culture

YouTube, TikTok, Instagram, and Facebook are wide open for track-specific creators. Share:

- Race breakdowns
- Sprint tips and form critiques
- Mic'd up workouts
- Meet day vlogs
- Injury recovery stories
- Scholarship success interviews

Monetize through:

- Ads
- Brand partnerships
- Affiliate links
- Paid memberships
- Digital products

Creators like this often make $1,000–$10,000/month depending on consistency and niche.

Track Meet Organizing

You don't need to run the AAU to get paid off meets.
Host a local invite, all-comers meet, or themed summer series.

Charge $10 per athlete.
Get 200 athletes = $2,000 in one day.
Bring in vendors, sell T-shirts, or livestream the meet for extra revenue.

Two meets per season = $5K+ side hustle that also builds community.

Nil Branding & Recruitment Support

If you know the track recruiting system, you can teach families how to navigate it.
Offer 1-on-1 sessions helping athletes get seen, build social media, email coaches, and present highlight reels.

Charge $200–$500 per consulting package.
Guide them through NCAA rules, timelines, and D1 vs D2 differences.

You can also help high school and college athletes monetize through:

- NIL brand building
- Custom merch
- Social media setup
- Deal negotiation coaching

Referee, Event Staff, or Official Roles

Certified meet officials get paid to start races, manage events, record results, or marshal athletes.

Most officials earn $100–$250/day depending on the meet.
Work 2–4 meets/month and you can earn an extra $8K–$12K per year, while staying active in the sport.

Speed Training Outside Of Track

Here's the compound effect: every sport wants speed.

Football, baseball, soccer, volleyball—all benefit from explosive movement.
Position yourself as a speed and agility specialist, and you open your income beyond the track.

Charge by the session or offer seasonal packages.
Partner with local coaches or schools to get client flow.

Compound Track Blueprint Example

Let's say you train 8 clients a week at $75 = $2,400/month
Host 3 camps/year = $9,000
Sell a $40 course that moves 300 copies/year = $12,000
Drop branded merch = $6,000/year
Shoot content that brings in $500/month = $6,000
Run 2 meets = $5,000

That's over $40K–$50K a year, sideline-built, athlete-led, and completely independent.

Closing Reflection

The clock will always matter. But the value behind the scenes is where wealth lives.

The problem isn't that people can't run.
It's that no one ever showed them how to run their business off the track.

Tierre Ford

You don't need gold medals to get paid.
You need a lane, a voice, and a system.
You already have the hustle. Now you have the blueprint.

"Track doesn't end when the race ends. The sideline has money, meaning, and momentum—if you're smart enough to build from it."

Chapter 34

Her Lane — Women, Mental Health, and Mindset in Track and Field

"She ran fast, but not to escape. She ran to remind herself she could stay in the race—on her terms."

Track and field has always produced some of the most iconic female athletes of all time—Flo Jo, Jackie Joyner-Kersee, Gail Devers, Allyson Felix, Shelly-Ann Fraser-Pryce, Sha'Carri Richardson, Sydney McLaughlin.

But behind every highlight is a truth rarely discussed:

Mental health is the other finish line. And far too many women cross it bleeding.

Because for every gold medal, there's performance anxiety.
For every PR, there's self-doubt.
For every IG highlight, there's exhaustion, isolation, and pressure to be perfect, polished, and unbreakable.

The Weight Of Being "The Strong One"

Female athletes—especially Black and Brown women—are often expected to carry everything:

- School
- Family trauma
- Social judgment
- Image management
- The pressure to "represent"
- And the unspoken rule: never break down in public

And when you're fast? Talented? Winning?

No one asks how you're feeling.
They only ask, "What's your next time?"

The system teaches silence. Push through. Shake it off. Cry later.

But that silence has broken too many women.

The Layered Pressure Of Identity

Women in track don't just run—they **carry**.

They carry body image issues.
They carry hypersexualization and erasure.
They carry the stigma of being "too muscular," "too masculine," or "too emotional."
They carry hair politics, media bias, and fake support that disappears when they're not winning.

Sha'Carri Richardson spoke it.
Allyson Felix lived it.
Simone Biles echoed it across all sports when she said, "No medal is worth my peace."

This isn't just about sport.
It's about safety, rest, boundaries, and healing.

The Mental Toll Of Always Competing

Track is different from other sports.

It's not team-first.
It's hyper-individual. Every split, every false start, every slow finish—it's all on you.

Now add:

- Limited Income
- No Union
- Constant Travel
- Little Downtime
- Coaches Who Don't Believe In Therapy
- Social Media Attacks
- And The Pressure To Keep Sponsors Happy Even While Grieving

That's not performance. That's **survival**.

Signs Of Mental Fatigue In Female Athletes

- Withdrawing from teammates or coaches
- Anxiety before meets
- Panic attacks during training
- Constant body comparison
- Depression after "off seasons"
- Overtraining to avoid feeling "lazy"
- Internalized shame for being "too soft"
- No longer enjoying the sport—but feeling trapped in it

What Mindset Really Means

Mindset isn't just motivation.
It's **recovery**.
It's **self-forgiveness**.
It's letting go of perfection.

It's asking for help without apology.
It's defining your success beyond medals and applause.

Some of the strongest female athletes in the world don't need to learn how to go harder.
They need to learn how to breathe.

Building Systems Of Mental Wealth

Here's how women in track are rewriting the script:

- Hosting "run and release" wellness events—no timers, just movement and community
- Creating therapy-centered coaching programs
- Starting group chats for athletes off the clock
- Launching podcasts to talk about the real stuff: heartbreak, injury, anxiety, body image, motherhood
- Designing journals for mindset prep instead of just race plans
- Partnering with therapists who specialize in sport trauma
- Speaking out—loud, raw, and honest—on what healing really looks like

Spotlight Story: Nia Samuels — Running For Peace, Not Points

Nia was a three-time conference champ in the 400m at a small D1 school. By junior year, she had sponsorship dreams, Olympic hopes, and a training schedule that pushed her six days a week. Nobody knew she was breaking inside.

She developed anxiety. Her periods stopped. She stopped eating right. She started hiding.

By the time she graduated, she didn't even want to touch a track.

But she came back—differently.

She started hosting free "Recovery Runs" in her city. No clock. No pressure. Just movement, breathwork, prayer, and music. She wrote a mindset workbook for Black female athletes called Run Light, Run Loud. She created safe spaces.

Now, Nia isn't just a former runner. She's a **healer in spikes**.

She makes $60K/year through courses, journals, speaking gigs, and community events. But more importantly, she's whole.

"I had to stop running from myself before I could run with love again."

Final Reflection

The game is changing.
But healing is the new hustle.

The strongest women on the track aren't the ones with the fastest times.
They're the ones who learn how to rest without guilt.
The ones who say, "Not today," and choose stillness.
The ones who redefine legacy through self-love—not self-sacrifice.

"Because the real finish line is peace."

Chapter 35

The Rise Of The Net — Inside The Numbers Of Volleyball's Climb

"She didn't just jump to spike. She jumped to rise—above expectations, into opportunity."

Volleyball is one of the most played women's sports in the United States—and one of the fastest-growing sports globally.

Across high schools, clubs, rec leagues, and beach tournaments, volleyball is creating more opportunities than ever for girls to earn scholarships, build brands, and compete at elite levels. But the truth is: **only a small percentage make it to the pros**. Even fewer earn livable contracts.

The game is growing. But the **business side is still catching up—** and that's where knowledge becomes power.

Youth To High School Pipeline

As of the latest data, there are over **470,000 high school girls** playing volleyball in the U.S.—making it the **second most popular sport for girls** behind track and field.

At the youth level (ages 8–14), participation is rising through **rec programs, travel teams, and club volleyball**—which is often **expensive but necessary** for exposure.

Many players train year-round through club ball, private lessons, and strength programs—all in pursuit of recruitment.

By high school, elite players are often traveling across states for tournaments and showcases, especially within **USA Volleyball, AAU Volleyball, and regional power leagues**.

Club Volleyball: Pay-To-Play Reality

To be competitive for college, most girls have to play club volleyball—which can cost **$3,000 to $10,000+ per year**, depending on the team, travel, gear, and fees.

This creates a barrier. Many talented girls never get seen—not because of skill, but because of financial limits.

Recruiting often favors players on big-name clubs, with exposure at national showcases, not just local tournaments.

College Volleyball Numbers

Out of nearly half a million high school players, only about **5.7% go on to play in college**:

- Around **1.2% play NCAA Division I**
- The rest split across D2, D3, NAIA, and junior college

Division I volleyball scholarships are competitive and often partial (except in elite programs).
 Players juggle heavy class loads, early weight room sessions, film study, travel, and constant performance pressure. There's also a strong international player presence—especially from Europe and Brazil—making D1 spots even more competitive.

The Pro Dream: Very Few, Very Thin

Here's the hard truth: **less than 1% of all college volleyball players go pro**.

And until recently, the **U.S. didn't even have a stable women's professional indoor league**.
Most elite players have gone overseas—to Turkey, Italy, Brazil, Japan—to sign short-term contracts.

Typical overseas pro contracts range from **$25,000 to $100,000/year**, with only **Olympians or top-tier players** earning more. Most contracts don't include long-term security, and many athletes live season-to-season.

Recently, two new U.S.-based leagues have launched:

1. **Athletes Unlimited (AU)** – a player-led league with a unique points system and media partnerships
2. **Pro Volleyball Federation (PVF)** – backed by big investors, focused on building regional fanbases

These leagues show promise—but are still early in development. Salaries range from **$35,000 to $65,000/year** in AU, with potential bonuses.

Beach Volleyball

Beach volleyball has its own path, including Olympic presence, AVP (Association of Volleyball Professionals) tours, and NCAA college teams.

However, **the earning gap is still large**, with most players supplementing income through clinics, NIL deals, coaching, and social media.

Injury Landscape In Volleyball

Volleyball may not have the bone-crushing collisions of football, but it's still physically demanding—especially on knees, shoulders, and fingers.

The most common injuries include:

- **ACL tears** (especially in women, due to biomechanics)
- **Ankle sprains** (from landing or foot contact under the net)
- **Rotator cuff and shoulder issues** (especially for hitters)
- **Overuse injuries** (from year-round training without recovery)
- **Finger fractures and jammed joints**

ACL tears are **2–4 times more likely in female athletes**, and a torn ACL can mean **9–12 months off the court**—sometimes ending a scholarship or recruitment pipeline.

The emotional toll of injury is also heavy: identity loss, isolation, anxiety about performance or return, and sometimes pressure to "just push through" pain.

Final Truth

Volleyball is one of the most **emotionally and physically demanding team sports** for women. The grind is real. The sacrifices are quiet. And for many players—after high school or college—it all ends with no real plan for what's next.

That's why we're not just here to break down stats. We're here to break open possibilities.

Because **even without going pro**, there are **lanes of income, leadership, and legacy** in this sport—and that's what comes next.

"The net isn't a barrier. It's a business line. Once you know what's behind it, you stop asking for a chance—and start creating your shot."

Chapter 36

Over The Net — Making Money In Volleyball Without Going Pro

"She may not play under lights anymore—but she still serves, still builds, and still gets paid from the game that raised her."

The dream of going pro is rare. But the power of the sport? That stays with you.

Thousands of former volleyball players aren't on national teams. They're not overseas in pro leagues. But they're making money—**coaching, training, building club teams, starting camps, dropping merch, and teaching the next generation how to move with strength and confidence**.

This chapter is about showing you **how to eat off the game**, even if your playing days are behind you.

Coaching And Private Training

Volleyball training is in demand—especially for girls ages 10 to 17.

Private coaches charge anywhere from **$40 to $100/hour**. Group training? Four girls at $40 each = **$160/hour**.

Train 10–15 players per week? That's $1,500+ a week.
 Multiply that by the year, and you're easily sitting at **$60K–$80K annually**, part-time.

Many players specialize in:

- Hitter mechanics
- Setting form
- Blocking and footwork
- First contact/passing drills
- Position-specific IQ training

Even if you weren't a pro, if you **played high school or college ball**, you can turn that into **a reputation, a business, and a waitlist**.

Camps, Clinics, And Pop-Up Events

Weekend clinics are where legacy meets income.

Charge $75 per player for a 3-hour skill session. Bring in 25 athletes? That's $1,875 in one day.
 Host 4–6 events per year and that's **$7K–$12K** just off seasonal offerings.

Add shirts, highlight videos, or lunch for more value.
 Run a "Mom & Me" clinic.
 Offer pre-season tune-ups or tryout prep camps.

The secret isn't perfection—it's **organization and community**.

Start A Club Or Micro-Academy

You don't need 12 teams to build a club.

Start small. One age group. One gym rental.

Monthly fees for club volleyball range from **$150 to $400+ per player**. With just one 12-player team at $250/month, that's $3,000/month in revenue.

Add uniforms, tournament fees, gear partnerships, and you've built a five-figure brand—while creating access for players in your city.

Content Creation And Education

Volleyball is one of the most under-served sports online when it comes to content. Start a TikTok, YouTube, or IG page and share:

- Coaching tips
- "What I Wish I Knew Before Club Volleyball"
- Mic'd up scrimmages
- Equipment reviews
- Tryout walkthroughs
- Player motivation

You can monetize through:
- YouTube ads
- Brand deals
- Paid digital products
- Affiliate links (Amazon, ball bags, shoes, ankle braces)

With the right niche, even 10K followers can bring in **$1,000 to $5,000/month**.

Merch And Lifestyle Branding

There's a growing market for volleyball fashion and empowerment gear—especially for girls and women.

You can create:

- Hoodies, tees, and socks with slogans like:
    - "Set Goals, Not Limits"
    - "Block Everything Negative"
    - "D1 Energy, Even in Practice"
    - "Volleyball Vibes Only"
- Custom kneepads or accessories
- Positivity journals for mental game prep

Use print-on-demand services. Start with low risk. Build through your local community and events.

NIL Consulting Or Mentorship

High school and college players often don't know how to:

- Build a personal brand
- Attract NIL deals
- Reach out to small companies
- Package their voice into a story that sells

You can teach them. Offer:

- 1-on-1 Zoom sessions
- Brand building templates
- "Pitch yourself" workshops
- Partnerships with local photographers for IG content

Charge $150–$300 per player or run group sessions.

Help five girls/month? That's a steady income while changing lives.

Officiating, Scorekeeping, Or Tournament Directing

You can also stay in the game as a certified ref, club tournament host, or event planner.

Refs earn **$25–$50 per match**, and full-day tournaments can bring in **$200–$300 per day**.

Organize a middle school invitational? A 12-team tournament with $250 entry fees earns **$3,000+ in one day**.

Add vendors, branded shirts, or livestreams and now it's a full-on business.

Spotlight Story: Coach Mia – The Setter Who Set Her Own Business Up

Mia played D2 volleyball in Indiana. She didn't go pro. But she knew how to lead a court—and how to teach girls to lead theirs.

After graduation, she started training three girls on Sundays. Word spread. By year two, she was coaching 20+ athletes per week, running tryout bootcamps, and hosting a "Confidence On and Off the Court" clinic every season.

She dropped her own brand, **"Set & Secure"**, with journals, crop tops, and volleyball planners.

Now she makes **$72,000 a year**, owns her time, and builds up girls who need more than just volleyball.

"I thought I was done playing. But I just had to change my role—from player to platform."

Closing Reflection

Volleyball doesn't end when the season ends.

It begins when you stop asking, "What now?" and start asking, "Who can I help? What can I teach? What can I build?"

Because even without pro status, you still have power.
 You still have an impact.
 And you still have value that people will pay for—if you move with purpose.

"You may have stepped off the court—but your game's not over. It's just getting started. Build your net. Protect your space. Serve your gift."

Chapter 37

The Fight For The Dream — Breaking Down Boxing From Youth To Pro

"In this game, you don't get ranked by followers. You get paid by what you survive—and who you become."

Boxing isn't just a sport. It's a story.
It's where underdogs get rich—or broken.
Where the ring becomes a home, a hustle, and sometimes a trap.

It's one of the most unforgiving athletic journeys in existence—but for those who understand the numbers, the grind, and the system, it's also a path to **power, respect, and wealth.**

Let's break down the game by the digits.

Youth & Amateur Pipeline

Every pro boxer starts in the same place—**a local gym.**

In the U.S., there are over **3,400 registered boxing gyms**, most of them serving low-income, working-class neighborhoods.

At the youth level, fighters usually enter between ages 8 and 14. They compete through:

- **USA Boxing** (the official amateur governing body)
- **Silver Gloves, Golden Gloves**, and other regional tournaments
- Local gym shows or exhibition matches
- Junior Olympics and AAU boxing circuits

By their late teens, serious amateurs may have **50–150 fights under their belt** before even turning pro.

But only a fraction ever go that far.

The Amateur Numbers

USA Boxing has roughly **50,000 registered amateur boxers**, across youth, junior, and senior ranks.

Only about **1% of those fighters turn professional**.
 Even fewer make it past **10 pro fights**, and even less ever headline a major card or secure a world title shot.

College boxing exists, but it's limited. Most fighters skip college and chase the dream through sparring, showcases, and small pro cards.

The Pro Fight Game

Once you turn pro, the numbers shift dramatically.

Entry-Level Pro Boxers:

- Typically earn **$500–$2,000 per fight**
- Must pay for their own trainers, cutmen, and travel
- Fight 4–6 times per year (if healthy and active)
- Often take short-notice fights just to stay relevant

They don't get sponsorships. They rarely have managers. They often fight injured.
 This is the reality of the **small hall** boxing scene—undercards, half-full gyms, chasing a payday.

Mid-Level Pros:

These are fighters with **10–20 wins**, possibly regional titles or TV exposure.

- They might earn **$10K–$30K per fight**, depending on promoter, venue, and ticket sales
- They may start getting attention from networks or streaming deals (DAZN, ESPN, Showtime)
- Most still work day jobs or train clients to survive between fights

Only a **handful break through each year** to sign with major promoters like Matchroom, Top Rank, or Premier Boxing Champions.

Elite-Level and Champion Fighters:

Once you reach the world stage—title holders, pay-per-view contenders, Olympians turned pros—the money gets real:

- **World champs can earn $250K–$2M per fight**, plus bonuses
- Top PPV stars (Floyd Mayweather, Canelo, Tank Davis, Jake Paul, Tyson Fury) make **$5M to $100M+** depending on opponent and platform
- Endorsements, clothing lines, and gym ownership become common secondary streams

But here's the truth: **Only about 30–40 fighters globally are consistently making million-dollar money**.

Everyone else? Still grinding.

Injury, Exploitation, And Burnout

Boxing is **extremely high-risk**. The injury rate is among the highest in all sports:

- Concussions and brain trauma

- Broken hands, ribs, and orbital bones
- Shoulder tears, neck and spine damage
- Long-term neurological damage (CTE)

There's no union. No guaranteed pension. No health care after retirement. Fighters often end their careers with:

- Zero savings
- Dozens of unpaid hospital visits
- Exploited contracts
- Broken relationships

Even former champs have ended up broke, brain-damaged, and forgotten.

Women In Boxing: Undervalued, Underpaid, Rising Fast

Women's boxing is growing, but still faces a massive pay gap.

Top female fighters like Claressa Shields, Amanda Serrano, and Katie Taylor have helped elevate the sport—earning **$200K to $1M per fight** on major cards.

But most women are still paid **a fraction** of what male fighters earn—with limited sponsorships, fewer televised cards, and shorter round times.

Still, they're showing up, showing out, and changing the system—one title at a time.

The Real Odds

Let's keep it real:

- 1,000 kids enter a gym
- 100 get through their first fight
- 20 go on a winning amateur run
- 5 turn pro
- 1 makes enough money to quit their job

- Maybe **one in 10,000 becomes a millionaire off boxing**

But for those who understand the game, boxing isn't just about fighting.

It's about teaching. Training. Branding. Managing. Commentating. Building gyms. Running media pages. Hosting events.

It's about learning how to **fight for your name and eat without getting hit**.

Spotlight Story: "Rico From Philly" — The Trainer Who Never Turned Pro But Built His Empire

Rico Thomas was a South Philly kid with fast hands and a chin that made grown men double-take. He had a 44–3 amateur record, two Golden Gloves titles, and a city that believed in him.

But he never turned pro.

At 21, his father passed. His mom needed help. He walked away from the ring.

For a while, he vanished—working construction, coaching part-time, getting by. But the fight was still in him.

At 26, he opened a tiny gym in the back of a barbershop. Six heavy bags. One ring. No heat. He called it **"No Excuse Boxing"**.

At first, it was just the neighborhood kids. Then came the high school athletes. Then came the parents, the teachers, even the cops.

Rico started training fighters—but more than that, he trained discipline, identity, protection, purpose. He taught girls how to walk with power. He taught boys how to cry without shame. He trained single moms, ex-cons, prep school kids, and city workers all in the same ring.

He didn't have a belt. But he had **impact**.

Today:

- Rico trains 80+ clients a week
- Runs five youth outreach programs
- Hosts an annual "Fight for Peace" charity card
- Launched his own merch line: **"Chin Down. Hands Up. Life On."**
- Makes over **$120,000/year** from coaching, camps, and partnerships
- Built a lane with no manager, no promoter, and no cut to give up

"I didn't need Vegas lights to be great. I needed a basement, a mouthpiece, and my city behind me."

"I still bleed boxing. I just stopped needing to prove it in the ring."

He never went 12 rounds in front of the world.
But every day, he steps in and **fights for somebody's life**.

"The real champs don't always wear belts. Sometimes, they wear bruises from building everybody else up."

"You don't have to take punishment to stay in the ring. You just need to know how the business works—and where your value lives."

Chapter 38

Outside The Ring — The Blueprint To Eat Without Taking A Hit

"Some fighters throw punches. Others throw plans. Both get paid—the smart ones just last longer."

The Money Behind Boxing

Globally, boxing generates **$1.1 to $1.4 billion annually** across pay-per-view, ticket sales, merchandise, betting, and sponsorships.

Men's Boxing

- Men dominate the PPV space. Top-tier male boxers like Canelo Alvarez, Tyson Fury, and Gervonta Davis are earning **$10M to $100M per fight**, including backend bonuses.

- Pay-per-view sales for one major fight (like Mayweather vs. Pacquiao or Canelo vs. GGG) can gross **$300M–$600M** in one night.

- Sponsorships, liquor brands, and apparel deals push elite boxers into **$150M+ net worth territory**.

But again—this is the 1%.

Women's Boxing

- Women have been systemically underpaid.
- Even world champs may earn **$20K to $300K per fight**, unless they headline a major event.
- Fighters like **Claressa Shields**, **Katie Taylor**, and **Amanda Serrano** are pushing the pay ceiling, with high six- and low seven-figure paydays becoming more common—but still not equal to the men.
- The good news: women's boxing is trending up, fast. DAZN, ESPN, and Showtime are all investing more screen time and better contracts.

The takeaway?

Boxing is a billion-dollar beast—but you don't have to be in the ring to get your cut.

The Blueprint: How To Get Money Without Getting Hit

Here's how real people—like Rico from Chapter 36—build real revenue outside the ropes.

1. Open a Community-Based Boxing Gym

It doesn't have to be flashy.

All you need:

- A small warehouse or rec center rental
- 6–10 heavy bags
- A few mitts, gloves, and speed ropes
- One or two assistants
- And your rep in the community

Charge $125/month for unlimited access.
50 members = $6,250/month = **$75,000/year**

Offer:

- Youth development classes
- Women's self-defense
- After-school sessions
- Conditioning for athletes
- General fitness bootcamps

Rico started in a barbershop basement. Now he makes six figures training everyone from soccer moms to aspiring pros.

2. Run Workshops, Camps, and Clinics

Weekend workshops = fast money and local impact.

Charge $50 per person.
30 people = $1,500 in one day.

Themes:

- Intro to Boxing: No Experience Needed
- Jab, Hook, Hustle (for teen boys)
- Hit Without Hate (anti-bullying youth sessions)
- Trauma + Training (women's confidence clinic)

Do it monthly. Promote on IG. Partner with schools or nonprofits.

Stack these events, and you're now in **$20K–$30K territory annually**—without any prizefighting.

3. Sell Branded Merch (Real Grit, Real Culture)

Start with:

- T-shirts
- Hoodies

- Hand wraps
- Duffle bags
- Hats or fitteds with hard slogans

Examples:
- "We Don't Flinch"
- "12 Rounds of Faith"
- "Chin Down, Life Up"
- "No Ref Needed"

Print-on-demand services like Printful let you launch without inventory.
 Even selling 100 shirts a month at $25 = $2,500/month = **$30K/year** side hustle.

Attach it to your gym or training page and it becomes a lifestyle brand.

4. Train Fighters and Fitness Clients

Don't just focus on boxers.
 Train:

- Football players who need footwork
- Women looking for cardio
- Teens building confidence
- Runners who need explosiveness
- Regular folks who want to feel powerful again

Charge $50–$100/session
 10–15 sessions/week = **$2,000–$5,000/month**

You can also create:

- Online boxing fitness programs
- Downloadable 30-day shadowboxing guides
- YouTube channels for technique and motivation

This is **scalable**, and can lead to sponsorships, speaking gigs, or even books.

5. Host Events, Tournaments, and Fight Nights

Partner with local promoters or host your own:

- Amateur fight nights
- Exhibition matches
- Spar-a-thons for charity
- "Black Tie Boxing" upscale events

Sell 200 tickets at $25 = $5,000

Add vendors, concessions, raffles, and local sponsors

Run 2–3 events/year and you're adding another **$10K–$20K** to your ecosystem.

6. Become a Media Voice

Create content:

- Gym vlogs
- Mic'd up mitt work
- Fight breakdowns
- "Lessons from the Corner" podcast
- Docu-style training stories
- Interview local legends and lost fighters

Monetize through:

- YouTube ads
- Patreon supporters
- Affiliate links
- Sponsored gym features

In boxing, **authentic voices get loyal audiences.**

Even 5,000 consistent followers can create monthly income and brand partnerships.

Real Blueprint: Rico's Breakdown (No Gloves Needed)

- Gym membership revenue: $6,500/month = $78,000/year
- Weekend workshops (6/year): $9,000
- Branded merch: $20,000
- Private clients: $25,000
- Youth contracts with nonprofits: $12,000
- Fight night co-promotion: $15,000

Total: $150K+ a year
No punches. Just purpose.

Final Reflection

The ring made legends.
But outside the ropes? That's where **legacy lives.**

You don't have to fight for respect—you just have to move like a business.
Train others. Build your name. Protect your community. Turn your gym into a lighthouse.

You don't need a title belt to feed your family.
You need a blueprint. And now you've got one.

"Some throw hands. Some throw hope. But the ones who throw systems—they build empires nobody can knock out."

Spotlight Story: Tasha "Too Real" Morgan – From Fighter To Founder

Tasha Morgan was known in Detroit's east side gyms as "Too Real."
She could punch through pads and people, but what set her apart was her footwork and focus. She went 32–4 as an amateur. People thought she'd go pro. She thought so too.

But after a bad decision loss at Nationals and a torn rotator cuff, the contract offers slowed.
The money dried up. And for the first time, Tasha felt invisible.

So she pivoted.

Instead of chasing promoters, she chased purpose.

She opened **Too Real Boxing & Wellness** in a strip mall next to a fried fish joint.
 Five heavy bags. One Bluetooth speaker. No mirrors—on purpose. She said, "You ain't here to look cute. You here to get real."

Tasha created something different:

- A trauma-safe boxing space for women and girls
- Daytime sessions for survivors of abuse and former inmates
- Night classes for single moms
- A mentorship program where teen girls learned how to throw combos and resumes

Then she launched **"Fight Like a Woman"**, a merch line and training series that went viral.

Now?

- Tasha trains over 60 people per week
- Runs three pop-up events every season
- Contracts with the city to teach boxing at juvenile centers
- Earns over **$110,000/year** from training, partnerships, and digital sales
- And she never took a single pro fight

"The ring didn't reject me. It redirected me."

"I stopped fighting to prove I was worthy. I started fighting to show others they are."

Tasha didn't win a world title.
She **built a world that saved lives**. And in the fight game, there's no prize more real than that.

"She didn't just lace up gloves. She laced up generations"

cashing out without ever getting KO'd.

Chapter 39

Beyond The Bell — The Money In UFC, Pro Wrestling, And The Hustle After The Hype

"They gave their body to the crowd. Now they're giving their mind to the money. The real fight was never in the cage—it was in what came after."

The Combat Money Tree

Combat sports aren't niche anymore. They're billion-dollar empires built on hype, pain, and personality. And whether you're watching Dana White yell post-fight or a pro wrestler jump off a table, just know—**money is moving fast in all directions**.

Ufc: The Fight Game, Rebranded

Mixed Martial Arts (MMA), led by the UFC, has grown from underground cage fights to a mainstream powerhouse. The UFC was purchased by Endeavor for $4 billion in 2016. Now it generates **over $1.3 billion annually**.

That includes:

- Pay-per-view (PPV) sales

- ESPN+ streaming deals
- Gate/ticket revenue
- Sponsorships (Monster, Crypto.com)
- Merch and licensing
- International fights (Abu Dhabi, Brazil, UK)

But the problem? **Fighters don't see most of that.**

UFC Fighter Pay Structure:

- **Entry-level UFC fighters earn $10K–$20K per fight.**
- Mid-tier fighters earn $30K–$100K per fight.
- Top-tier stars (Israel Adesanya, McGregor, Jon Jones) can make $500K to $5M+ with bonuses and PPV shares.

But most UFC fighters:

- Fight 2–3 times a year
- Pay 10–30% to coaches, managers, and gyms
- Get no healthcare or retirement
- Can be cut after one loss
- Can't wear personal sponsors due to UFC's exclusive deal with Venum and others

So they hustle outside the octagon.

Pro Wrestling: The Theater Of Combat

Pro wrestling isn't fake—it's scripted combat. And the money is **very real**.

WWE (World Wrestling Entertainment) generates over **$1.3 billion per year**, with AEW (All Elite Wrestling) closing in at **$100–150 million annually** and growing.

Money flows from:

- TV rights (NBC, FOX, TBS)
- Pay-per-view events
- Merch (shirts, belts, collectibles)

- Licensing (video games, toys)
- Live tours
- Social media and YouTube (WWE has over 96 million subs!)

Wrestler Pay:

- **WWE entry-level salary**: $50K–$150K/year
- **Main event talent**: $500K–$3M/year
- **Legends and crossover stars** (The Rock, Cena): $5M+ per appearance

AEW pays slightly less, but allows **more brand freedom** and **outside partnerships**.

The Mental And Physical Toll

Whether it's UFC or WWE, these athletes give **everything**—and often walk away with:

- Broken bones
- Torn ligaments
- CTE
- Depression, identity loss
- Addiction
- No financial plan

That's why more fighters are now **owning their brand** and building beyond the ring.

Blueprint: How They're Getting Money Outside The Fight

1. Open a Gym or Academy

From jiu-jitsu to fitness boxing, MMA fighters are launching training centers:

- $100–$250/month memberships
- Private lessons at $100+/hour
- Weekend fight prep clinics

Build a loyal base, and you're looking at **$60K–$200K+ per year**, with merch and programs on top.

2. Start a Podcast or YouTube Channel

Fighters like Brendan Schaub, Michael Bisping, and even Logan Paul built entire media businesses:

- Fight commentary
- Training advice
- Interviews
- Behind-the-scenes stories

Monetize through:

- YouTube ads
- Patreon
- Brand sponsorships
- Merch drops

Even a 20K subscriber base can bring **$2K–$10K/month**.

3. Create Your Own Fight Promotion

Fighters like Jorge Masvidal (Gamebred FC), Khabib (Eagle FC), and Jake Paul (Most Valuable Promotions) have flipped the game.

They:

- Promote new fighters
- Stream their own events
- Sell tickets and merch
- Build long-term equity

You can start smaller—local smoker events, regional tournaments, charity cards.

4. Monetize Your Name, Moves, and Merch

Signature sayings, walkout gear, wrestling names—it's all IP (intellectual property).

Launch:

- "Never Tap Again" gloves

- "Choke God" grappling tees
- "Walkout Warrior" supplement brand
- "Pin Her Down" fitness plans

You don't need 1M followers. You need **consistency, story, and service.**

5. Teach What You Know: Courses, Mentorship, Mindset

Turn your journey into a system:

- 8-week "Fight Like a Champ" training plans
- "Grit & Glory" women's self-defense programs
- Wrestling for Beginners: The Hustle Behind the Slam

Sell online or in-person. Price at $97–$497.

Build a real passive income lane off your **life experience**.

Spotlight Story: Erik "No Lights" Santiago – The Guy Who Got Paid After The Bell

Erik fought 12 pro MMA fights. No TV. No fame.
His biggest payday? $2,000 and a busted jaw.

At 29, he was done. But not defeated.

He opened **Humble Savage MMA** in a rundown Detroit gym.
Started training five kids. Turned it into 50.
Then launched a YouTube series on "How to Stay Dangerous After Retirement."

Now?

- He trains 100+ fighters a week
- Runs 3 amateur fight cards per year
- Has 20K YouTube subs
- Just inked a collab with a supplement brand

"I thought the fight was the peak. Turns out, it was just the proving ground."

"I got punched for 10 years so I could speak without fear for the rest of my life."

He didn't headline a UFC card.
He **built a city around his story**.

Closing Reflection

This ain't just about belts.
It's about **blueprints**.

You may never headline a pay-per-view.
But you can headline your community.
You can build your brand, teach your struggle, monetize your message—and do it all without leaving the game bloody.

Because the real fight isn't between fighters.
It's between **your old self and your next self**.

"Fighting gives you discipline. Now use it to build. Let the crowd go. Build your corner. The bell already rang—it's your

Chapter 40

Motivational Speech: "Write Your Own Highlight Reel"

Your coach can scream at you.
Your mama can pray over you.
Your mentor can hand you the blueprint.

But if you don't lace your shoes, step up, and apply it—
None of it matters.

See, information is **just potential**.
Books don't build businesses. Action does.
Dreams don't cash out—**discipline does.**

You got the blueprint?
Then **pick up the hammer.**

Because the difference between a highlight and a regret?
One got filmed.
The other got forgotten.

You think you need luck?
You think you need a last name, a rich cousin, or a shoutout from somebody famous?

Nah.
You need to move like your unborn children are watching.
You need to suffer like your name is the only bridge **between the street and salvation**.

And when it gets hard—and it will—
You remember names like:

Rayna Jefferson, who took a torn hamstring and built a track empire from scar tissue and faith.
Rico from Philly, who never saw Vegas lights, but turned basement sweat into six-figure legacy.
Tasha "Too Real", who turned pain into power, and gloves into gospel.
Erik Santiago, who left the cage but stepped into purpose—no promoter, just vision.

They didn't wait for a scout.
They didn't need permission.
They **scouted themselves**.

Let me give it to you straight:
You want the cheat code?

Apply it.
Repeat it.
Stack it.
Don't quit.

That's the **compound effect**.
That's the real hustle.
That's **how you win invisible battles before anyone knows your name**.

Perseverance + Purpose = Legacy.

Tierre Ford

You're not here to watch others win.
You're not here to repost someone else's moment.
You're here to be the one who made it.

So stop spectating.
Start executing.

Write the vision.
Fund the dream.
And start filming your own highlight reel—one move at a time.

Because when the credits roll on your life,
You better not be a background character in your own story.

Chapter 41

Plan Like A Boss — Building A Real Business Strategy

"A vision without a plan is just a hallucination. And a dream without a deadline is just a wish."

Let's be clear: hope doesn't fund businesses. Hype doesn't pay the bills.

You can have all the passion in the world, but if you don't have a real strategy? You're running a sprint with no finish line.

So this chapter is your compass. Your layout. Your architectural draft for whatever empire you're building. Because your hustle deserves more than adrenaline. It deserves structure.

1. Know What You're Building (Clarity Over Chaos)

You don't need to have everything perfect. But you do need to define what you're doing. Is it a brand? A service? A movement? A local training camp? An online product? A mentorship platform?

Write it down: What problem are you solving?

Be clear. Real clear.

"Helping people get in shape" is vague.

"Helping Black fathers over 30 lose weight with boxing-style fitness routines they can do at home in under 30 minutes" is crystal.

Specificity is power. If people can't repeat your vision in one sentence, you don't know it well enough.

2. Pick Your Model (Keep It Lean, Keep It Real)

There are only a few ways to make money:
- Sell a product
- Offer a service
- Create content and monetize it
- License your skills
- Get sponsorships or partners

You don't need to do all five. Start with one. Build your model like you're stacking bricks, not gambling chips.
Ask:
- How much does it cost me to run this per month?
- How much can I charge per sale/session/client?
- How many customers do I need to break even?

Break-even isn't failure. It's foundation.
From there, scale smart. Don't chase every opportunity. Multiply what works. Eliminate what drains you.

3. Name It Like You Mean It

The right name carries weight. It doesn't have to be fancy, but it should be memorable, mission-driven, and aligned with your identity.
Some tips:
- Keep it short (2-3 words is best)
- Avoid hard-to-spell names
- Check for domain/social media availability
- Make it personal, but scalable

Examples:
- "Fight Forward Academy"

- "Built Not Bought"
- "Urban Seed Training"

Don't wait six months to launch because you're stuck on the name. But don't treat it lightly either. Your name introduces you before you speak.

4. Craft the Offer (This Is Your Real Currency)

Your offer isn't just what you do. It's what people experience.

You're not selling a t-shirt. You're selling confidence, alignment, identity.

You're not just running a youth camp. You're giving parents peace of mind and kids a taste of structure and self-respect.

Define your offer like a heavyweight jab:

- What are you solving?
- Why should they trust you?
- How do they pay? (Subscription? One-time? Tiered?)

People pay for outcomes, not effort.

So paint the outcome.

5. Set Your Price With Guts, Not Guilt

Stop underselling yourself because you're new. Or scared. Or trying to please broke-minded people.

Your price should reflect:

- The problem you solve
- The result you deliver
- The energy it costs you to do it

You can always discount later. But start with value.

"If you don't respect your price, nobody else will."

Charge for the transformation, not just the time.

6. Map the Month (Create 30-Day Sprints)

Forget five-year plans. That's for corporations.

Right now? You need 30-day movement.

Ask yourself every month:
- What are my income goals?
- What products/services am I pushing?
- What events or content will I release?
- How am I building my audience?

Keep it simple:
- Week 1: Build
- Week 2: Promote
- Week 3: Sell
- Week 4: Evaluate and adjust

Business is rhythm. The more consistent your moves, the more predictable your money.

7. Know Your Numbers (Don't Hide From the Math)

Too many people stay broke because they're scared of spreadsheets. But your numbers don't lie.

Track:
- Total income per stream
- Expenses (monthly and per sale)
- Profit margins
- Conversion rates (views to buyers)

You don't have to be an accountant. But you have to be aware.

Know what feeds you. Know what drains you. Keep receipts. Stay audit-ready even when you're small.

Because broke hustle is loud. But smart hustle lasts.

8. Build a System, Not a Cage

You didn't start this to become your own employee.

Create systems that let you:
- Schedule content in advance
- Automate bookings or payments
- Use templates, not constant improvisation
- Delegate once you're ready (even part-time help!)

Freedom is the goal. Systems buy you time.

9. Remind Yourself Who You Are

When the doubt creeps in—and it will—remember:

You're not doing this just for likes. You're doing this for legacy. For the kid who needs a version of you in their city. For the community that's never seen ownership done right.

You are building what your younger self never got to witness. That's purpose. That's pressure. That's holy.

So write the vision. Plan the move. And walk like your blueprint already got buyers.

Because real bosses don't just hustle.

They orchestrate.

Chapter 42

Fund The Hustle — Getting Capital Without Selling Your Soul

"Your dream isn't too expensive. Your strategy just needs better execution."

Let's break the myth now: **You don't need to be rich to get started.** You need to be **resourced**. You need to be **intentional**. And above all, you need to know how to **move with precision** in a system designed to overlook the unprepared.

This chapter is your map to money that doesn't own you. No soul-selling. No 30% interest loans. Just real, proven paths to **fund your dream while keeping your power.**

1. Shift Your Mindset: From Scarcity to Strategy

Don't say "nobody gives out loans to people like me." Instead ask: **"Who is giving out loans to people like me, and what do they require?"**

Don't say "I don't have the credit." Say: **"Let me build my credit blueprint now."**

Money follows movement. Resources follow research. If you believe the capital doesn't exist for your business, it never will. But if you prepare like it's coming, and pitch like it's yours to lose? You'll find yourself inside rooms you never thought would open.

2. Start With the Free Money: Grants

Yes, **free money exists**. But it doesn't go to vague dreams. It goes to people who can prove they're ready.

Look into:

- **Local city or county business grants** (especially for minority-owned startups)
- **Nonprofit partnerships** (like Black Business Boom, Digital Undivided, and Operation HOPE)
- **Corporate-backed grants** (FedEx Small Biz Grant, SheaMoisture Fund, NAACP partnerships)
- **Pitch competitions** (recorded or live)

Tip: Create a "Grant Folder" with:

- 1-pager business summary
- Headshots or logo
- Pitch video (60-90 seconds)
- Basic budget
- Mission/impact statement

Apply monthly. Make it routine. Five no's and one yes could still mean **$10K you didn't have before.**

3. Microloans That Work (Not Predatory Traps)

These are small loans meant to help you start or stabilize your business without putting you in debt quicksand:

- **Kiva Loans** (0% interest, crowdfunded, up to $15K)
- **Grameen America** (for women entrepreneurs)
- **Accion Opportunity Fund** (loans starting at $5K with flexible terms)

- **Community Development Financial Institutions (CDFIs)**

Pro Tip: CDFIs are the hidden gems of Black entrepreneurship. They want to work with people like you. But you must come correct.

Bring:

- Your business plan
- Realistic repayment plan
- Proof you're already doing something

4. Banking Smart: Build the Profile Before the Ask

If you walk into a bank today and say "I got a dream," you'll walk out with a smile and a decline letter.

But if you've:

- Registered your business name
- Opened a business checking account
- Separated personal and business funds
- Made consistent deposits (even small ones)

Then 6–12 months later, you have proof of performance. Add in:

- Clean bookkeeping (use Wave, QuickBooks, or even Excel)
- EIN number and DUNS registration (for business credit)

You just became **a safe bet**.

5. Pitch With Purpose: Tell the Right Story

Nobody funds your idea. They fund your execution. And if you want to stand out? **Pitch like you already believe you're the answer.**

Hit these beats:

- **Problem:** What gap are you solving?
- **Proof:** What have you done already?
- **Plan:** How will this money scale you?
- **People:** Who do you serve, and how does this matter?

Practice your pitch. Record yourself. Refine it. Confidence can raise more than capital. It raises belief.

6. Crowdfunding Without Begging

GoFundMe is good, but GoBuildMe is better. Set up a real campaign:

- Use **Kickstarter** or **Indiegogo** for products
- Use **IFundWomen** or **FundBlackFounders** for ideas with impact

Tell your story. Offer value. Give people a reason to sow into you beyond pity.

You're not asking for help. You're offering investment in a vision.

7. Collaboration Over Competition

Sometimes your best funding is **partnerships**.

Example:

- Start a youth sports camp but **partner with a therapist**, a nutritionist, and a school district.
- You don't need to be the expert in everything.
- Build a proposal together and apply as a collective for grants.

Community builds credibility. Collaboration builds capital.

8. Protect Your Energy, Not Just Your Assets

Every "no" is not personal. But every "yes" should be intentional. Don't take money that demands your soul, waters down your mission, or owns your brand.

You want **investors**, not buyers. You want **partners**, not puppeteers.

This is still your legacy.

Final Word: Start Small, Think Eternal

The money is out there. The system isn't always fair, but the cracks are wide enough for the prepared.

Every grant you apply for, every loan you research, every document you organize—it's not busy work. It's battle prep.

You don't have to wait until you're "ready." **You get ready by moving.**

And remember:

"A dollar with vision is louder than a million with doubt."

Chapter 43

Build While Broke — The Compound Effect Of Daily Discipline

"You don't need a budget to be dangerous. You need a reason to keep going when nobody's clapping."

Let's talk about what most books, coaches, and social media gurus won't: **starting from broke.**

Not low-budget. Not underfunded. **Broke.**

Broke like:

- Still owe on last month's rent
- Keeping your old logo because Canva Pro costs too much
- Hustling Wi-Fi from your cousin's house just to upload your pitch deck

If that's you, **good.** Because it means you're still in the fight. And this chapter isn't about shame. It's about **strategy.**

This is where we show you how to build **from the ground, without pity**. Where we stack small wins, dial in daily moves, and use the **compound effect** to outlast every doubter who counted you out.

1. Embrace Your Starting Line

Your story doesn't start at success. It starts in survival. And that's **nothing to hide**.

Stop waiting to get polished before you get started.

If you got:

- A phone
- A voice
- A story
- And a work ethic

Then you have everything you need to **start showing up**. Daily.

You don't need funding to be consistent. You need **focus**.

2. Time Is Currency: Spend It Like Rent Is Due

If you're broke financially, then **your time is your investment capital.**

You can use it:

- To learn skills (YouTube University is free)
- To grow visibility (Instagram, TikTok, Twitter)
- To build content (write, post, film, design)
- To email, DM, network

If you're binge-watching shows but claiming you're broke, you're not broke. You're **avoiding the work.**

Budget your hours like money. Cut out waste. Put your effort in the most **revenue-facing activities** possible.

3. Stack Micro Wins Like Brick and Mortar

You don't need a viral moment. You need a **repeatable system of small wins** that build momentum.

Examples:

- 1 new follower per day = 365 potential customers in a year
- 1 cold DM per day = 7 pitch opportunities per week
- 1 post per day = 30 brand touches a month

Keep a **Compound Win Journal.** Log every step.

What gets tracked gets duplicated. What gets duplicated builds trust. And trust turns into **income.**

4. Use Free Tools Like You Own Them

Being broke forces creativity. That's your superpower. Here are free tools you should be using right now:

- **Canva** (design, content, pitch decks)
- **Google Docs/Sheets** (business plans, trackers, SOPs)
- **Mailchimp or ConvertKit Free Plan** (email lists)
- **Linktree/Beacons** (free landing pages)
- **TikTok/IG Reels** (free marketing with viral potential)
- **ChatGPT** (brainstorming, writing help, idea generation)

Don't wait for a software budget. Use the free versions **ruthlessly**. Make them work for you until you can upgrade.

5. Learn Skills That Reduce Your Burn Rate

If you can't afford to outsource, **insource your grind.**

Learn:

- Basic branding + design (YouTube: "Canva branding tutorial")
- Website building (Wix, Carrd, or Notion for free landing pages)
- Social media management (use free scheduling tools)
- Video editing (CapCut is free)

You're not wasting time learning. You're investing time that will **save you thousands**.

Once you earn more, outsource **intentionally**. But in the beginning, **wear every hat proudly.**

6. Be So Consistent It Becomes Your Reputation

You might not have a marketing budget. But if people know:

"They show up every day."

That's a currency. That's a reputation. And that reputation becomes value.

Because one thing broke creators often overlook is **trust**. If your audience doesn't trust you to stay consistent, they won't trust you with their money.

Consistency = credibility.

Credibility = conversion.

7. Bet on Content You Can Create, Not Imaginary Campaigns

You don't need a brand agency. You don't need $5K for a photoshoot.

You need to turn your truth into **content**:

- Story videos (tell why you started)
- Transformation breakdowns (how you've grown)
- Education gems (give value)
- Client feedback/testimonials
- Behind-the-scenes: the process is the brand

Start with what you have:

- That $50 logo? Make it iconic.
- That cracked iPhone camera? Shoot with it until it pays for a better one.

Perfection is the enemy of earned growth.

8. Build a Broke-Proof Morning Routine

If your money is unstable, your habits have to be unshakable.

Suggested blueprint:
- **6:30 AM:** Wake up (don't hit snooze)
- **6:45 AM:** 10-minute reflection (prayer, journaling, mindset)
- **7:00 AM:** Stretch + review day's top 3 tasks
- **7:30 AM:** Free learning (1 video, podcast, or blog post)
- **8:00 AM:** Attack the highest-priority income-producing task

Win your morning, and you control your day.

Discipline is how broke becomes booked.

9. Sell Like Your Story Depends on It

Don't say you're bad at sales.

You sell every day:
- Your ideas to friends
- Yourself to employers
- Your opinions online

So why not sell your brand?

Learn how to:
- Make an offer
- Ask for the sale
- Follow up without shame

Nobody's psychic. If you don't ask, they won't know what you offer.

Be clear. Be bold. Be **about your business**.

10. Know That Broke Ain't Your Final Chapter

This is not your end. This is your **origin story**.

Every movement started with somebody being broke, fed up, and ready to build. Every great business had a day when the founder ate noodles and bet on a dream.

You are in your building phase. You are earning your future with discipline today.

So don't fold. Don't scroll yourself into paralysis. Don't let shame slow your strategy.

You are not small. You are simply **at the bottom of your greatness.**

And the only way out? **One honest, consistent, hungry, God-fueled move at a time.**

From Silence To Spotlight — Alicia's Voice

Alicia grew up with a stutter. She hated speaking in class, never imagined herself in business, and certainly didn't see herself on camera. But when she launched her handmade skincare line, something shifted.

She filmed a video anyway. Her hands trembled. Her voice cracked. But her story was real.

"This started because my eczema made me ashamed to be seen. So I made something that made me feel whole."

That video got 38,000 views. Orders flooded in. Now she trains others in authenticity marketing.

(Napoleon Hill): "Strength and growth come only through continuous effort and struggle."

The Lost Son Turned Local Legend — Dre's Redemption

Dre did five years for a crime he didn't commit. Came home bitter. Parole-bound. Unemployable.

So he picked up a camera. Started filming local AAU games. At first, for free. Then $25. Then $200 a clip.

In two years, he built one of the hottest highlight pages in his city.

"I never played D1. But I helped three kids get seen and signed. That means more."

Quote (John Hope Bryant): "You build wealth from your story, your purpose, and your impact."

The Dance Floor Teacher — Rosa's Pivot

Rosa was a dance instructor in a school that shut down during the pandemic. She thought her journey was over.

Then she started teaching choreography on Instagram. Not just moves—she taught confidence, rhythm, and self-esteem. She built a global community of 70K women.

"Dance gave me my body back. Now I give that back to others."

(Suz Tuz): "Your story is the most valuable thing you own. Use it like it's gold."

Broken Back, Unbreakable Brand — Malik's Fight

Malik had a football scholarship. Until the tackle that shattered his spine. While recovering, he started writing about discipline. First it was posts. Then a blog. Then he turned it into a brand.

Now he sells fitness journals, teaches mental toughness, and speaks at schools.

"The pain didn't ruin me. It refined me."

(Bruce Lee): "Do not pray for an easy life, pray for the strength to endure a difficult one."

Fired, Then Fueled — Sam's Blueprint

Sam lost her corporate job. No warning. Just a pink slip.

Instead of collapsing, she documented the whole journey: Day 1 of job loss. Day 5 of freelancing. Day 20 of pitching her brand.

Her transparency went viral. She launched a content creation masterclass and became her own boss in under six months.

"I stopped asking, 'Why me?' and started asking, 'What's next?'"

(Michael Jordan): "I've failed over and over and over again in my life. And that is why I succeed."

Closing Reflection: Your story isn't your shame. It's your strategy. What you survived is someone else's roadmap.

So tell it. Share it. Build with it.

Because your voice is more than content—it's currency.

Chapter 44

Market With Heart — Your Story Is Your Superpower

KEYNOTE BREAK

How To Build The Next Chapter Of You

1. Write It Down (Define the Mission)

- What are you building?
- Why does it matter?
- Who is it for?

Before the LLC. Before the logo. Before the launch. You have to be brutally honest about what you're building.

Is it a brand, a business, a movement, or a mission? If you can't explain it clearly to a 12-year-old in under 30 seconds, keep refining.

Clarity is the foundation of strategy.

2. Create a Vision Board

- Physical or digital—see your brand, goals, and audience

- Use images, quotes, key numbers, and logos to train your mind

Make your vision visual. Not just in your head—in your face. Every time you pass by it, your subconscious gets the memo. This isn't a dream. It's a plan.

Use tools like Pinterest, Canva, or old-school scissors and glue. Build a board that shows who you're becoming.

3. Craft Your Business Plan

- What do you sell?
- Who pays for it?
- How much does it cost to run?
- What problem do you solve?

You don't need a Harvard MBA. You need real answers to real questions.

Your business plan can start as:

- A simple Word doc
- A mind map
- A pitch deck with five slides

But it must be honest.

Where are you now? Where are you going? And what does it take to get there?

A vague plan invites confusion. A clear plan attracts capital.

4. Learn to Fund It (Grants, Loans, Partnerships)

- Use CDFIs, local Black-owned business grants, SBA microloans
- Build a clean 1-page pitch with brand story + numbers
- Network with intent—your next investor might be one handshake away

Research is free. Courage is free. Initiative is free. Start with what's available in your zip code. Reach out to local chambers, nonprofit business incubators, and small business development centers.

Your first $500 doesn't have to come from your pocket. It can come from a pitch, a partner, or a program.

It's not about who has the money. It's about who has the readiness to receive it.

5. Never Give Up (Track Your Compound Wins)

- Every new customer = a win
- Every email sent = momentum
- Every tweak = elevation
- Every rejection = redirection

Track your wins like they're gold.

Keep a notebook. A spreadsheet. A notes app. Every action you take toward your dream counts.

One post. One pitch. One "yes." The power isn't in going viral. The power is in going daily.

Consistency is louder than hype. Discipline is your silent partner.

Closing Reflection:

You are not waiting on motivation. You are building your future with quiet moves.

You don't have to be famous to be effective. You don't need millions to be meaningful. You just need clarity, consistency, and a willingness to bet on yourself.

Write the vision. Execute the plan. Walk like it already belongs to you.

Chapter 45

The Builder's Blueprint

From Idea To Identity — Writing The Vision With Fire

"You don't become legendary by thinking it. You become legendary by writing it down, building it up, and living it out."

This is the pivot. The shift. The moment where this book stops being words and starts being your new instruction manual.

From here on out, we're not dreaming anymore. We're drafting. We're not just inspired. We're intentional. We are not imagining success. We are becoming the architects of it.

1. Define Your Brand Voice (Speak Like You Know Who You Are)

Your brand voice is how your business would talk if it were a person.

Ask yourself:

- Is your brand streetwise and gritty?
- Is it warm and nurturing?

- Is it bold and cutting-edge?

Pick 3 adjectives to guide your tone. Are you "authentic, sharp, motivating"? Or "playful, edgy, unstoppable"?

Exercise: Write a mock Instagram caption, a 30-second elevator pitch, and a response to a customer complaint—using your brand's voice.

If your tone feels forced or inconsistent, go back to your roots. Real always sounds better than rehearsed.

2. Identify Your Mission and Core Values

A brand without a mission is a car with no destination.

Ask:

- What problem are you solving?
- What pain are you removing?
- Who are you doing it for?

Then write your mission in one sentence.

Example: "To equip first-generation entrepreneurs with real-world tools and confidence to build profitable, purpose-led brands."

Now define your top 3–5 core values. Some options: Integrity. Innovation. Community. Discipline. Transparency. Joy. Freedom. Excellence.

Your values aren't marketing fluff. They're anchors. They keep you from chasing trends.

3. Create Your Audience Avatar

You are not for everyone. And that's a superpower.

Create one ideal customer profile with these questions:

- Name?
- Age?

- Gender?
- Pain points?
- What do they dream about?
- What keeps them up at night?
- What are they scrolling for?
- What do they want that they don't have?

Give them a story. Make them real. If you speak to everyone, you connect with no one. But if you speak directly to one, the right many will follow.

4. Vision Board Prompts

Get tactile. Get visual. Whether it's a poster on your bedroom wall or a Pinterest board on your phone, see the version of you you're becoming.

Prompts:

- Your ideal workspace
- A logo that speaks to you
- Brands you admire (what do you love about them?)
- Inspirational quotes that keep you grounded
- Screenshots of positive feedback or milestones

Train your brain to expect success.

5. Drafting Your Logo and Tagline

Your logo doesn't need to be perfect today. It needs to be clear and consistent.

Pick a symbol, wordmark, or font that aligns with your voice. Choose 1–3 colors and stick to them across all platforms.

Tagline: Write a 3-7 word phrase that says what you stand for.

Examples:

- "Built for the Underdogs"
- "Move Different. Win Louder."

- "Legacy Over Likes"

Don't overthink it. Your tagline is your banner. Let it wave.

6. The Clarity Checklist

Before you build further, check yourself:

- Do I know my brand's tone?
- Do I have a mission statement?
- Do I know who I'm serving?
- Do I understand what problem I solve?
- Do I have visual inspiration?
- Do I have a logo or sketch?
- Do I have a working tagline?

If you answered "no" to any of those, pause and go back.

Clarity isn't a luxury. It's a requirement.

This Is Your Turning Point

You're not just someone with a good idea. You are a brand in motion.

You are shaping identity. You are designing legacy. You are applying fire to blueprint.

"The moment you name the mission, you become more than a dreamer. You become a builder."

Now, let's keep building.

Chapter 46

Behind the Game — The Final Hustle Play

"If you knew how much money moved behind the scoreboard, you'd stop watching and start building."

Let's not play with it. Let's not whisper. Let's close out this section the way we lived it: with facts, fuel, and fire.

This chapter is your final push. The recap. The reality check. The roadmap. You don't have to go pro to get paid. But you do have to move like the opportunity already belongs to you.

Recap By Sport: What You Might Have Missed

Football

- Annual Revenue: $19+ billion (NFL alone), billions more in high school, college, and youth
- Sideline Hustles: Coaching, refereeing, sports videography, training camps, podcasting, NIL management, equipment sales

Basketball

- Annual Revenue: $10+ billion (NBA), with hundreds of millions more across NCAA and AAU
- Sideline Hustles: Tournament hosts, NIL agents, personal trainers, content creators, videographers, jersey/apparel printers

Baseball

- Annual Revenue: $11 billion+ (MLB), plus minor leagues, college ball, Little League
- Sideline Hustles: Private hitting coaches, league directors, tournament merchandisers, media archivists, scorekeepers

Golf

- Annual Revenue: $84 billion U.S. golf economy
- Sideline Hustles: Course maintenance, pro shop owners, online instructors, junior league builders, club designers

Tennis

- Annual Revenue: $6+ billion global market
- Sideline Hustles: Private coaches, youth club operators, event streamers, tennis bloggers, gear testers

Track & Field / Volleyball / Boxing / MMA / Pickleball / Soccer

- Combined Revenue: $100+ billion in global value
- Sideline Hustles: Athletic therapists, trainers, gym owners, tournament promoters, sponsorship consultants, analytics and data firms

Total Combined Revenue Potential

From youth to pro, across every level and every lane:

Over $250 billion annually in the United States alone. Globally? Over $700 billion in the sports economy.

And less than 1% of that money goes to players.

The rest?

- Coaches
- Media teams
- Tournament directors
- Brand consultants
- Stat collectors
- Equipment techs
- Social content teams

That's your lane. That's your opportunity.

Your Hustle Motivation: Time Is On Your Side

Time is your cheat code. Your leverage. While others waste it scrolling, you could be:

- Writing eBooks
- Training youth
- Starting a sports media page
- Filming athlete reels
- Designing the next big brand

"You don't need a timeline. You need a lifeline. One you build yourself."

Start with one lane. One hour. One yes. The compound effect does the rest.

Your Final Playbook — Real Money Moves

- Launch Something Local: Tournaments, clinics, leagues
- Sell the Knowledge: Courses, books, webinars, guides
- Create the Content: Podcasts, video reels, highlight tapes
- Serve the Athletes: Brand building, media training, consulting
- Partner & Pitch: Schools, sports tech startups, local gyms

Closing Words: The Legacy Is In the Hustle

Let them play. Let them score. Let them shine.

You? You're building behind the curtain. You're the director. The architect. The owner of impact.

The scoreboard gets the headlines. But the sideline makes the money.

The game is big. But your vision is bigger.

Now go own your piece. Build it. Brand it. Teach it. Flip it. Grow it.

Legacy is a verb. Start moving.

OTHER BOOKS BY TIERRE FORD

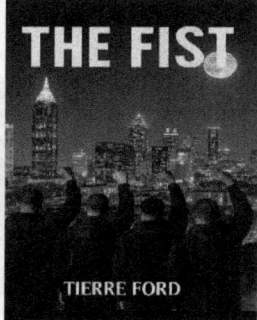

Tierre Ford

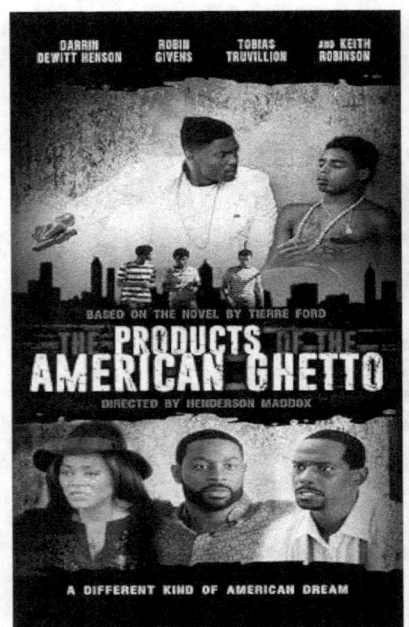

www.ingramcontent.com/pod-product-compliance
Lightning Source LLC
Chambersburg PA
CBHW050338010526
44119CB00049B/594